HOOK 'EM WITH HUMOR

The Public Speaker's Guide
to Having Fun and Using Humor
to Mesmerize, Fascinate, and Engage

RICKY OLSON

PEACOCK PROUD
P·R·E·S·S

Hook 'Em with Humor: The Public Speaker's Guide to Having Fun and Using Humor to Mesmerize, Fascinate, and Engage

Copyright © 2017 by Ricky Olson

First Published in the USA in 2017 by Peacock Proud Press
ISBN 978-0-9981212-2-2 paperback
ISBN 978-0-9981212-3-9 eBook

Library of Congress Control Number: 2017934398

All rights reserved. No part of this publication may be reproduced, stored in or introduced into a retrieval system, or transmitted, in any form, or by any means (electronic, mechanical, photocopying, recording or otherwise) without the prior written permission of the publisher. This book is sold subject to the condition that it shall not, by way of trade or otherwise, be lent, resold, hired out, or otherwise circulated without the publisher's prior consent in any form of binding or cover other than that in which it is published and without a similar condition, including this condition being imposed on the subsequent purchaser.

Book Cover:
Judith Mazari, www.judithmazari.net

Portrait Photographer:
Elaine Kessler, www.elainekesslerphotography.com

Editors:
Laura L. Bush, Ph.D. www.laurabushphd.com
Nina Shoroplova, www.ninashoroplova.ca

DISCLAIMER:
This is a work of nonfiction. The information is of a general nature to help readers know and understand more about humor. Readers of this publication agree that Ricky Olson will not be held responsible or liable for damages that may be alleged or resulting directly or indirectly from their use of this publication. All external links are provided as a resource only and are not guaranteed to remain active for any length of time. The author cannot be held accountable for the information provided by, or actions resulting from accessing these resources.

My Dear Karen, I love you. Thank you for your tireless support and encouragement. Our 26 years of marriage have been an amazing blessing.

I'll never forget the day we met when our eyes locked across the room. Although I knew immediately what I wanted, I'm forever grateful that you broke the ice. My heart still skips a beat whenever I recall the way you said, "Welcome to McDonalds. May I take your order?"

AAAhhh! The voice of an angel. You've forever "super-sized" my life.

Testimonials/Advanced Praise

"In the world of professional speaking, the well-worn question, 'Do you have to be funny when giving a talk?' is quickly followed by the equally well-known response, 'Only if you want to get paid.' In this highly readable yet highly researched work, Rick Olson has something for everyone. Whether you're a novice or a newcomer to our speaking arena—or even a seasoned pro—you will find a treasure trove of great content spiced with practical and usable ideas. "So, welcome to our world! In short order, you'll be 'hooked with humor!'"
Edward E. Scannell, CMP, CSP, Past National President, National Speakers Association. Co-Author, *Games Trainers Play* **Series (McGraw-Hill), Scottsdale, Arizona**

"Perhaps an oxymoron, but this is a serious book about humor. Ricky's practical, serious, and fun approach to humor reminds me of the first humor seminars presented by the National Speakers Association in the 1970s by Dr. Charles Jarvis. I highly recommend this book, not only for speakers, but for the thousands of marketing professionals whose presentations to customers determine their income."
Don Thoren, CPAE Speaker Hall of Fame, Class of 2009, Legends of the Speaking Profession, and professional speech coach. Tempe, Arizona.

"*Hook 'Em with Humor is an essential read for ANY speakers looking to make a high impact with their audience, captivate and hold their attention, and most importantly, have fun doing it!* Rick teaches you all the how-to's of including humor in your talk, even if you don't feel like you're that funny. He also shows exactly why humor makes you more compelling to event organizers dying to have someone entertain their audience and make them look like rock

starts for finding you. LOVE THIS BOOK!"
Kristen Nolan, Motivational Speaker and High Performance Health Mentor, www.kristennolan.com

"Rick clearly takes being funny seriously—and he knows what he's talking about! Of course, you don't have to just take his word for it, since this well-crafted guide is full of proven research and expert corroboration. As a corporate leader and professional speaker myself, I've applied Rick's lessons and seen results, whether I was talking to 3 people or 3,000. It's clear that this book can help speakers like me plan and deliver funnier material. The results are more gigs, more fans, and more repeat business—and that's no laughing matter."
Julie Holmes, Award-Winning Speaker and Strategy Expert, julieholmes.net

"Hook 'Em with Humor *is full of it—humor, personal stories, practical advice on how to develop humor, tools to improve our presentations, tips on how to overcome challenges, and resources for further development. It is a must read for the seasoned speaking professional as well as the novice.*"
Danny Valenzuela, Professional Member, NSA, Certified Professional Coach. Certified Team Performance Coach

"Hook 'Em with Humor *is equal parts research and hands-on practical exercises designed to improve your ability to use humor to engage with your audience. Every great public speaker knows how critical it is to get a laugh at the very start and throughout a speech. If you mistakenly evolved a belief that you simply aren't funny and can't learn to be, Ricky blows that misconception out of the water. Anyone can learn to be funny using Ricky's practical advice. In addition to a comprehensive literature review on the subject of humor, I especially appreciated the 90-day humor improvement*

plan. It is possible to wake up your dormant funny bone! I highly recommend Hook 'Em with Humor *for any trainer or speaker who wants to improve the audience experience.*"
Lisa Maurer, Performance and Learning Consultant. Professional Member, NSA

Acknowledgments

This book would not have been possible without my wife Karen's love, support, and the quirky smile she throws my way when I share the weirdness I'm thinking. Thank you.

A good editor is hard to find. Thankfully, I found one. Thank you, Laura, for your encouraging and kind approach to letting me know how much editing needed to be done without really saying how much editing needed to be done.

Apparently, a lot of editing needed to be done because Laura called in reinforcements. Thank you, Nina, for providing the final polish my manuscript needed to be first-class.

Without Toastmasters® International, Toastmasters District 3, and specifically, Tempe Toastmasters, I wouldn't have gained the experience needed to develop the tools and processes in this book. Thank you, fellow Toastmasters.

Thank you to those who braved reading the first few drafts and for providing feedback: Don, Ed, Lisa, Danny, Kristen, and Julie.

Thank you, Laura, for not only being my editor, but for wanting to be the publisher. I appreciate your enthusiasm for what you do. Plus, thanks for all the laughs with you and Julie from Influence Publishing on our video chats as we worked through many publishing and promotion details.

Sometimes life can get in the way of our plans. When that happened to me, Ricardo showed up in a big way wearing a cap. Thank you. Thank you!

And finally, to my mentor, my coach, and my friend Jerry Corley, thank you! You are a true coach. I'm amazed watching you bring out the very best in people. I know you can do that because you can see each person's very best. You are gifted beyond measure.

Contents

Testimonials/Advanced Praise V
Acknowledgments IX
Foreword XV
Introduction 1
How to Use This Book 7

Chapter 1: When Being Naturally Funny Failed Me 13

Chapter 2: The 5 Obstacles to Using Humor and Being Funny 19
The First Obstacle—Mindset 19
The Second Obstacle—Being Willing to Practice and Do the Work 21
The Third Obstacle—Beware the Vagueralities 23
The Fourth Obstacle—No Access to a Great Teacher, Coach, or Mentor 25
The Fifth Obstacle—Techniques and Tools but No Applicable Process 26

Chapter 3: Humor Demystified 29
But What Should You Practice? 30
Why Do People Laugh? 30
Review 32
Time to Practice 33

Chapter 4: The Laugh Generator™ Process 39
The Laugh Generator™ Process 42
The Process in Action 45

Chapter 5: The 7 Reasons Humor Is a Must or You Fail 49
Laughter Benefits Your Audience 50
Grab Your Audience's Attention 52
Keep Your Audience's Attention and Ensure They Are Listening 53
Help your Audience Remember and Learn 54

Encourage a Willing Mindset in Your Audience..55
Help Your Audience Know, Like, and Trust You 55
How Making Your Audience Laugh Benefits You 56
A Bonus Reason to Use Humor—Event Organizers Want It....................58

Chapter 6: The Simple Joke Writing System™ 61
Combining Ideas to Get Even Bigger Laughs 62
Generate Custom Laughs 65
The Process 69
Writing Exaggeration Jokes...70
Writing a Rule of Three Joke 71

Chapter 7: The Laugh Multiplier™: Turning One Laugh into Many 73
Tags/Toppers 73
How Are Tags/Toppers Created? 75
Act-Outs 77
Callback...79

Chapter 8: The 7 Deadly Humor Mistakes Speakers Make and How to
    Avoid Them 81
Mistake #1—Not Using Humor or Trying to Ignore Its Important Benefits..81
Mistake #2—Using Street Jokes, Book Jokes, or Canned Jokes 82
Mistake #3—"Borrowing" Someone Else's Jokes 82
Mistake #4—Being Impatient and Giving Up Too Soon..............................83
Mistake #5—Not Testing Out Material Ahead of Time 85
Mistake #6—Writing for the Page and Not the Stage 86
Mistake #7—Starting Out by Asking, "What Is Funny?" 87

Chapter 9: Delivery and The Laugh Amplifier™ 89
Tone 90
Pacing and Speed 91
Pause Timing—The Art of the Pause 92

Volume	92
Enunciation and Articulation—Speak Clearly	93
Facial Expression	93
Body Language and Gestures	94
Is It Okay to Laugh at Your Own Joke? Absolutely!	96

Chapter 10: The Laugh Troubleshooter™ Process	99
Are All the Right Words in the Right Places?	100
Did You Give All the Necessary Facts?	101
Did You Leave a Little Puzzle the Audience Needs to Solve?	102
Are You Leaving the Interpretation up to the Audience?	105
Is the Twist at the End?	105
Is the Surprise Too Far Away?	106
Did You Talk Over the Laugh?	107

Chapter 11: The Unfortunate Truth—Why You Aren't Funnier	111
How Your "Funny Bone" Develops	113
Chicken Sexing, British Aircraft, and Being Funny	115

Chapter 12: The Safe Humor Solution™	119
Target	119
Know Who YOU Can Joke About	120
Be Certain Who Your Target Is	121
Know Who Your Audience Is Okay Joking About	122
If in Doubt, Joke about Yourself	122
Subtext	124

Chapter 13: Where to Add Humor	127
Your Bio	127
Your Speech Title	127
Your Introduction	128
Your Opening Remarks	129

Your Stories and Anecdotes 131
Your Closing 132
How Much Humor? 133

Chapter 14: The Material Machine™: Finding More Humorous Content. 135
Ad-Libs 135
Audience Interaction 138
The Event 139
The Event Location 140
The Speech 144
Related Quotes and Clichés 144
Stories Related to the Themes and Points of Your Speech 145
Your Life 146
Daily Events 147
Your Audience 147
Current Media 148
Time of the Year 149

Chapter 15: The Writer's Block Eradicator™ 153
How to Do It 156

Chapter 16: Putting it All Together 161

Resources 169
What Now? 169
Becoming the Funniest You 172
The 90-Day Humor Improvement Plan™ 184

Author Bio 191
Notes 193

Foreword

As a comedian for nearly thirty years, and as a writer and a comedy coach, I've spent most of my life studying comedy—how it affects performance and how it can be used in presentations, teaching, ministry, scripts, and casual conversation. I understand comedy's power to help an audience retain information as well as capture their attention, whether in casual conversation or in front of a huge audience. Comedy gets people to like you. No, wait. To LOVE you!

That's right. Love. When we laugh, our brain releases serotonin, oxytocin, vasopressin—all the feel-good hormones our body releases when we fall in love. That chemistry is also, by the way, the same chemistry released when we shoot heroin. So when they say laughter is the best medicine, they mean it in more than one way!

All kidding aside, laughter has immense power. It can get you a job over the candidate who is your competition. It can get you a sale from a skeptical customer. It can get an audience to trust, confide in, and vote for you (if that's what you want). It can get you a girlfriend or a boyfriend. Actor-rapper Will Smith says that all the girls he ever dated liked him because he had a sense of humor.

I love getting under the hood to study humor. And I mean really study why people laugh. It's an obsession for me. Go figure! I was one of those kids who used to take apart his toys to discover how they worked. Usually the only thing I discovered was that I couldn't get the toy back together again.

A sense of humor is one of those things that people mistakenly view as "you either got it or you don't." One of the reasons for this misconception is that the study of humor is relatively new. When you start reading Hook 'Em with Humor

XVI | Hook 'em with Humor

by Ricky Olson, however, you'll understand that humor is a skill. And, by definition, a skill can be taught. Early on in my own comedy career, I developed a reputation for being able to take anyone and make them funny—on one condition: they had to do the work!

Several years ago, I met Ricky Olson when he was looking for a coach to help him with his stand-up comedy. I've never seen anyone work harder than Ricky. He dug in and worked like he was hungry to learn. I immediately recognized that he already had a well-developed sense of humor. What he needed to learn was how to harness humor, so that at will, he could use the power of comedy whenever he was speaking in front of people—not just when he was being funny at lunch with his pals.

Ricky liked the way I broke down the humor process, first by describing why someone laughs, which I call "laughter triggers." Then I taught him—and many, many others—how to use the major comedy structures to intentionally pull those triggers and make people laugh, no matter what kind of material is being delivered. Ricky was so dedicated to learning more about humor that he would travel with his wife back and forth from Phoenix, Arizona to Burbank, California for my weekend writing workshops and my 8-week stand-up classes. He'd even repeat classes multiple times because once he understood that comedy was a skill that could be learned, he knew it could be learned faster through deliberate practice.

Because of Ricky's dedication and practice, he learned faster than anyone I've ever had in my class. In fact, he won the district humorous speech contest for Toastmasters (no easy achievement). Then he got booked for his first corporate gig just 18 months after he started with me. In one night at one corporate gig, Ricky made what most people would be proud to make for a week's worth of work.

Ricky's continued success led him to write a book on how to develop your own sense of humor. What better way to learn than from someone who went through the exact experiences he shares with you in his book? Hook 'Em with Humor is a perfect cumulative approach for anyone who wants to learn to apply humor in his or her speeches and presentations. The book combines personal knowledge and experience with valuable advice from experts in the field of comedy who have paved the road before us. If you're looking to develop your skill in adding humor to your speeches, then Hook 'Em with Humor is the exact type of book I'd recommend.

Finally, there's one reason this book works. Ricky has put in the work! I enjoyed reading it. I hope you do too!

Jerry Corley
Comedian, Writer, Teacher
www.standupcomedyclinic.com

Introduction

This book is for you, the professional or aspiring professional speaker. Don't tell me you aren't a professional speaker. You can try, but I won't believe you. In fact, I'll put my hands over my ears, shake my head, and yell, "blah, blah, blah, I can't hear you!" Exactly who is a professional speaker? Everyone! And I'm not the only one who feels this way. Author and presentation expert, Timothy Koegel shares the same view in his book, *The Exceptional Presenter*:

> Adopt a broader definition of "presentation skills" to include any form of oral communication. I frequently hear the following comment, "I only present once or twice a year. I don't use these skills very often." That's not true.
>
> Every time you open your mouth to speak in public, you are a public speaker.[1]

As you rise to speak and take an actual stage, you have your audience's attention. (Especially if you trip and fall, but pratfalls aren't a great way to start a speech.) For at least the length of time that you speak, you can hold their future. But you face a challenge: How do you engage with your audience, connect with them, and influence them so that they will take your message and ...

And what? Exactly!

What do you want your audience to do with what you are sharing? Tell me you want more than just polite nods and claps. Most likely, you want them to buy into your message and take action. In some cases, that means donating to your cause, investing in your product, or acquiring a new, life-changing outlook on life. Talking about new, John Morley (1838-1923), British statesman, explained that only three things matter in a speech: **who** says it, **how** they say it, and **what** they say. Of the three, Morley said what you say **matters the least**

To effectively influence your audience, you must capture and hold their attention and be memorable. In a good way. Like a bowel of hot soup (yum, soup) on a cold day, making you feel cozy, warm inside. That's a good way to be memorable. In his book, *Tame the Primitive Brain: 28 Ways in 28 Days to Manage the Most Impulsive Behaviors at Work*, Mark Bowden shares this intriguing example:

> A young, eager executive gave his first presentation to senior management. Although he did what he could, when the lights came on, and he asked, "Any questions?" he wasn't prepared for the response. He faced the CEO snoring away at the head of the table. Thankfully, the CEO didn't wake up when the presenter chucked the laser pointer at him and left the room in a cloud of unpleasantries.[2]

Yes, I know this may seem like an extreme example, but it's not too far from the truth for most of us. Timothy Koegel says, "80% of presenters are below average, 10% are average, 5% are good to very good, and 5% are exceptional. Bottom line: if you want to get exceptional results, then you need to be an Exceptional Presenter!"[3]

What does it mean to be an exceptional presenter? Let's consider one of the most popular presentation platforms of our time, the TED Talk. According to TED.com, the organization is founded on a few key principles: "the inspired format, the breadth of content, the commitment to seek out the most interesting people on Earth and let them communicate their passion."[4] According to Carmine Gallo in *Talk Like TED*, TED videos are being viewed over 1.5 million times a day.[5] The most popular TED Talk? Although there's some debate,

Entrepreneur author Kim Lachance Shandrow lists Ken Robinson in the number one position.[6] Robinson's top position is backed up by the TED.com's playlist entitled, "The most popular talks of all time."

So what's the secret to education advisor Sir Ken Robinson's popularity? Laughs. That's right. He generates a lot of laughter in his audience. From a recent *Business Insider* article, author Carmine Gallo (*Talk Like TED* and *The Storyteller's Secret*) wrote, "In the first five minutes of his speech, Robinson gets about 10 laughs.... At two laughs a minute, that makes [his] talk funnier than the movie *Anchor Man* (1.6 laughs per minute) and on par with *The Hangover* (2.5 laughs per minute)."[7] Why does Sir Ken generate so many laughs in his presentation? Simple. He believes in laughter's power to hold an audience. In the book *Storyteller's Secret*, Sir Ken says, "If they're laughing, then they're listening."[8]

Ensuring your audience is listening is just one of the many benefits of laughter. Robinson's quote is referenced everywhere on the Internet related to public speaking and humor. And equating laughter with listening is powerful. It's definitely powerful (and convenient) if you're writing a book on using humor in presentations. But what he says next is just as powerful: "If I'm laughing, I'm relaxing."[9] In other words, laughter has the power to help the audience and the presenter. It helps everyone have fun. To ensure presenters understand the value of humor, I devote an entire chapter to the research-backed benefits of generating laughter in your audience.

Here's the bottom line: If you want to be an above-average speaker, you simply must use humor. In nearly every book on presentations and speaking, the writer includes the same obligatory mention and regurgitated advice about how the best speakers are funny. Every author recognizes humor is essential to speaking. But just including a few paragraphs or a chapter about humor is not enough. Humor is so powerful to the art of speaking that it deserves its own book. Just one book though, the one you're reading. No others, okay? Promise me I'll be your one and only.

But what, you ask, if you don't think you can be funny?

Don't panic. Help is on its way. Regardless of how funny you are (or are not), you can learn to be funnier and add humor to your speeches and presentations. How do I know? Well, I'm considered to be naturally funny and being "naturally funny" failed me. Through that journey and my own learning process, I discovered that being funny wasn't some magical gift for a select few. Much to my own surprise I discovered that NO ONE is really "naturally" funny, not even me. (Learning that was hard to take. I still haven't recovered.) While studying and learning the skill of humor development, I realized that *anyone*—and I do mean *anyone*—can learn to how to get more laughs.

That means YOU can get more laughs, too.

But how do you do that? Some major obstacles stand in your way. I know because they stood in my way when I started in stand-up comedy and then again when I transitioned to humorous speaking. When I first tried stand-up comedy, I struggled. I didn't exactly "bomb" but I didn't get the laughs I expected. Even though I am naturally funny, my ability didn't easily translate to the comedy stage. I had to learn how to be funny. I nearly quit until I found a true teacher and coach.

I'll tell you how it happened in chapter one so you don't have to wait long.

Here's some great advice Bob Hope wrote in the foreword to Gene Perret's book, *How to Hold Your Audience with Humor: A Guide to More Effective Speaking*: "Humor is the welcome mat between the speaker and the audience. A short joke, a quick laugh, breaks the ice between you and that sea of strangers. When they laugh, they are immediately on your side. The laughter makes them your friends."[10]

How to Use This Book

I read a lot of books, and I'm often frustrated by the typical table of contents with chapter titles that provide no real glimpse into the chapter's actual content. Therefore, I've written "How to Use This Book" to provide you with specific places to start reading my book based on the content most relevant to you. Obviously, I think you should read my entire book, but if you're in a hurry, here's a handy guide to find what you need and want quickly.

If you don't think humor is necessary in every speech or presentation, go straight to "The 7 Reasons Humor Is a Must or You Fail" (chapter five). In that chapter, I provide (gasp! wait for it ...) seven reasons for using humor in every speech or presentation. Actually, in that chapter, I've added a bonus reason to use humor—more speaking gigs! All eight of these reasons are backed by research. I've included the references, so you can check out the research for yourself.

If you aren't convinced that it's possible for anyone to learn to be funnier, I totally understand how you feel. I used to think people could not learn to be funnier. You were either funny, or you weren't. But a couple of events changed the way I thought about being funny. If you're a skeptic like I was, you'll want to start by reading "Humor Demystified" (chapter three) and "The Unfortunate Truth—Why You Aren't Funnier" (chapter eleven).

In "When Being Naturally Funny Failed Me" (chapter one), I struggled to do well in stand-up comedy, even though from the time I was five years-old, people told me I was funny. In this chapter, you'll learn how a typical night out with my friends totally changed the way I thought about being funny. In "The Unfortunate Truth—Why You Aren't Funnier" (chapter eleven), I explain in great detail how natural humor can be developed and become part of your personality. I could have given this chapter the title, "How a Funny Bone Develops" because chapter eleven really looks at the brain science around implicit learning, implicit memory, and tacit knowledge, as well as how learning, memory, and knowledge are really at work when we say someone has a sense of humor.

Finally, in "Humor Demystified" (chapter three), I share the most important thing you can do to generate laughter. Although people laugh for a variety of reasons, you can learn how to intentionally cause people to laugh. No whoopee cushions or clown noses required. Once you learn how to do that one thing, you'll be on your way to becoming A Funnier You.

If you've tried being funny on stage before, but it didn't go well, start with "The 7 Deadly Humor Mistakes Speakers Make and How to Avoid Them" (chapter eight), where I explain several potential reasons your attempt at humor didn't go well and how to avoid those mistakes in the future. One common mistake I share about, for example, is not testing out your material. The last place you want to find out if something is funny or not is in front of a live audience. Believe me, I know. Blank stares from an audience feel like death; hence the term, "I'm dying up here."

If you like the idea of generating laughs, but aren't sure you can, read "The 5 Obstacles to Using Humor and Being Funny" (chapter two) and "Humor Demystified" (chapter three). In these chapters, you'll discover the concept of mindset and how modern neuroscience and research is discovering the reality behind how some people grow and achieve, while others don't.

If you'd like to generate laughs during a speech or presentation, but you aren't sure where it would be appropriate, read "Where to Add Humor" (chapter thirteen). Here, I list specific places that offer perfect opportunities for laughs. You may be surprised that a couple of the best places aren't even in your speech. You can start generating laughs before you even take the stage! From there, read "The Laugh Generator Process" (chapter four) to learn how to produce the laughs that are already in your speech but have been missing in your past presentations.

If people have told you that you're funny, so you aren't sure this book will provide any value for you, start with "When Being Naturally Funny Failed Me" (chapter one), where I talk about how I got started in stand-up comedy. However, when I wanted to transition to humorous speaking, neither being naturally funny nor my experience in stand-up really helped me. Then I recommend you read "The Laugh Generator Process" (chapter four). At the beginning of that chapter, I share how and why I had to take a different approach. I couldn't just rely on something that came "naturally" to me. Frankly, if you're someone who is "naturally" funny, you'll probably have an easier time following my processes. However, without the processes, you'll have a very difficult time trying to take your natural humor to the stage, if that's what you want to do.

If you've purchased other books or courses on being funny but aren't sure this book will provide any additional value, start with "The 5 Obstacles to Using Humor and Being Funny" (chapter two). There, you'll discover one of the major challenges I encountered on my journey: I had no foundational process for generating reliable humor. Although the books and some other courses I took provided tools, techniques, and formulas, I struggled without a process. Next read about "The

Laugh Generator Process" (chapter four). You'll quickly see that any of the practical, usable information you've acquired from those other books and courses will come alive within The Laugh Generator Process.

If you know how to write jokes or be funny but don't know how to come up with material, you'll want to jump right into "The Material Machine": Finding More Humorous Content" (chapter fourteen). Here, I identify all the opportunities that exist for discovering humorous content. Plus, I give specific examples to demonstrate how my humor-generating processes work to come up with material. From there, I believe you will also benefit from "The Writer's Block Eradicator" (chapter fifteen).

If you know how to write jokes but aren't sure how to perform them, start by reading "Delivery and The Laugh Amplifier" (chapter nine). That chapter is all about the essential components of delivering material to generate laughter. Best of all, because I give you an easy process to use, you'll be able to start practicing the components of delivery that produce the greatest laughs right away.

If you want to generate more laughs and get the most out of every laugh you are currently generating, go to "The Laugh Generator Process" (chapter four). By using this simple process, you will be able to generate laughs from your existing speeches and presentations. In this chapter, I show you how to stop missing out on these natural opportunities. You'll soon begin to see opportunities in every speech. From there, read "The Laugh Multiplier: Turning One Laugh into Many" (chapter seven), where I show you a process to turn every laugh you're currently generating into two, three, four, or more laughs. Next, you will want to read "Delivery and The Laugh Amplifier" (chapter nine). Here, I demonstrate how to get the most out of every laugh. You'll learn specific techniques to crank up the intensity of each laugh. This process will help you turn a two- to three-second laugh into a five- to 10-second laugh, or more.

If you are interested in writing some jokes for your speeches or presentations, start with "The Laugh Generator Process," which is, at its heart, the technique for writing jokes. From there, read "The Simple Joke Writing System" (chapter six). This simple system will open up the next level of joke writing for you.

If you have some jokes that work sometimes with some audiences but don't work at other times, read "The Laugh Troubleshooter Process" (chapter ten). You'll discover that there are only a couple of reasons your audience doesn't laugh. Once you know those reasons, you'll be able to walk through the process and discover the tweaks you need to make.

If you're worried about offending your audience with humor, I know exactly where you're coming from. Everywhere I looked online for help about adding humor to speeches and presentations revealed a scary, two-headed monster. On the one hand, humor is necessary, but on the other hand, it can be dangerous if you use potentially offensive material, so be careful. Read "The Safe Humor Solution" (chapter twelve) to understand the two elements of a joke, the target and the subtext. They're the two elements that are most often responsible for offending an audience. When you know and understand these elements, you'll be able to quickly identify whether a joke you're considering using has the potential to offend someone or not. The solution isn't to know your audience. The solution is to know your joke.

If you're looking for a magic formula to make you instantly funnier, I'm sorry, I've got nothing for you. All I have is a process and an offer that, if you're willing to put forth some real effort, you can be funnier on stage and off. But it will take work, serious work. Please take it more seriously than I took my first job washing dishes at the Elks Lodge. I don't know what they were complaining about the dishes were *mostly* clean. If you read one of the resources at the end of my book, "Becoming the Funniest You," you will understand how you need to practice, practice, practice to generate more laughs in your speeches or presentations. After reading "Becoming the Funniest You," take a look at the "The 90-Day Humor Improvement Plan" The plan will help you take all the information from my book and put you on a fast track to becoming A Funnier You in just 90 days.

If you want to see how to put it all together, check out chapter sixteen, where I share a real example of creating a humorous speech from start to finish. You'll have a "behind the scenes" view of the art, science, and process of being A Funnier You.

1.

When Being Naturally Funny Failed Me

As I sat at the tiny Starbucks table, I wondered what I had gotten myself into. I had thought that, since I was naturally funny, I could easily become a comedian. So I decided to give it a shot.

But, there I was and there it was, my empty notebook page staring back at me ... taunting me: "Whatcha got, funny guy?" I let out a sigh and took another drink from the Grande Americano with an extra shot. Boy, oh boy, I really needed that extra shot to kick in. And then I heard that familiar voice of doubt: "Maybe you aren't that funny after all. You only got voted second funniest in high school. Oh, and don't forget when your 'friends' insisted you enter the funniest person on campus contest in college and you got second—again!" Who could forget that?

I continued looking at that empty page, trying to figure out what was funny and willing myself to write something—anything—I began to seriously question and wondered, "What was I thinking?" My entire life I'd been told I was funny. My parents' friends compared me to the beloved character of Spanky in *The Little Rascals*. I actually laugh out loud while recalling one night while visiting another family, they proclaimed that we should stay for supper. While my parents were graciously trying to deny the invite (What were they thinking? They had great food), the man of the house declared, "You need to stay because I don't want to be eating this sh** all week." I barely missed a beat when my 10-year-old mouth quipped, "Well if it's sh**, I don't want to eat it now." Everyone laughed, even my mother laughed while trying to scold me at the same time.

As I took another slurp of my Americano, I remembered in college, my friends always encouraged me, "You should really be doing stand-up comedy," they'd say. "You are sooooOOOOO funny!"

And yet there I was, sitting in a Starbucks, staring at a blank page trying to write jokes. Now my mind has more evidence for how "I wasn't really good at anything," and this one really hurt because I was known as "the funny guy." It was my identity. "The funny guy" is who I am, and who everyone tells me I am, but at that moment, I couldn't think of a single funny thing to write! Another sip of coffee failed to java jolt my mind into thinking of something funny.

My mind started to wonder. I only even gave comedy a shot because I had stumbled into a free, introductory workshop to stand-up comedy. Heck, I thought to myself, if someone thinks they can teach comedy, I could probably learn it. But, as my blank notebook and I sat there, drinking coffee and struggling to write jokes, I felt like giving up.

Although the stand-up classes at the Tempe Improv challenged me, my biggest struggle was not knowing what the "instructor" wanted from me exactly. I was losing hope that a naturally funny guy like me would ever get paid to be funny. Although he offered an occasional "Nice joke!" or "I like where you're going with that," I also had to endure his always ambiguous and very frustrating coaching: "Write from more emotion. Highlight your setup and your punch lines."

As an obsessive person who loathes failure, I doubled my efforts. Thanks to the Amazon Kindle, my wife had no idea how many books I was buying. She did see my effort and the time I was putting into it, which encouraged me and helped my confidence a lot. Now I started searching the Internet for answers, any answers ... COME ON! While preparing for my third performance, I felt my frustration reach an all-time high. I finally reached out to a man in LA who offered one-on-one coaching by way of Skype. The part that caught my eye? He promised a "systematic way to write comedy faster."

What did I have to lose, right? He couldn't make me less funny, could he?

Within the first 10 minutes of talking to Jerry Corley, I knew I had found the essential piece that I had been missing and what I desperately needed: someone who knew what he was talking about when it came to comedy. Jerry was able to explain why people laughed (he called them the Laugh Triggers). He could also derive the basic joke structures that came from their laughter. Over a couple of Skype sessions, we worked together and created a really great set of jokes for my third showcase. Then the most unexpected thing happened. Only one month later, thanks to Jerry's coaching and mentoring, I got my first paid gig!

I was hooked—and hooked bad.

I drove to LA to take his weekend comedy-writing workshop. And then, a few weeks later, he started a new stand-up class on Saturday afternoon. Perfect! My wife supported me and drove with me over to Burbank on Saturday mornings. I would take Jerry's class, we stayed overnight in California, and then drove back home to Phoenix on Sunday mornings. We did that for eight weeks. The drive time was six hours each way. The hotel room ran about $129 a night. Plus, I paid for additional private coaching sessions with Jerry over Skype, more weekend workshops, and three additional eight-week classes. Yes, you're reading that right. I invested significant time and money to become good at stand-up comedy.

I believe that qualifies as doing the work—at least in part. In addition, I read more books, took improv classes, and joined Toastmasters. I was lucky to find a place to perform stand-up and improv regularly at a high-level for two, three, or four shows a week.

And then something I didn't expect to happen, happened.

I was with a large group of people at a restaurant having dinner being my usual funny self. People were laughing so hard, they couldn't breathe. I don't say that to brag, but to tell you that making people laugh wasn't an out-of-the-ordinary occurrence for me. This time, though, I noticed that, while I thought I was being my naturally funny self, I noticed that I was using one of Jerry's formulas. In fact, I had incorporated two or three formulas into what I was saying.

From that night forward, I started paying more attention to how I talked with my friends. Sure enough, whenever I was being "naturally" funny, at least one of those formulas or laugh triggers was present. I realized then that I could teach people to become more "naturally" funny. As a result, I started studying all the research on laughter I could find.

At the same time, I was still working to win the Toastmasters' District Humorous Speaking Championship. Finally, all the hard work paid off. In July 2014, I got my first paid headlining gig. And then in November, I won the District 3 Humorous Speaking Championship. Since then, I've been focused on refining the process of creating humor to help anyone quickly and easily add humor to their speeches and presentations. I've released two online courses: one for speakers and another for adding humor to dating profiles. I've taught several workshops on both those topics as well, and I've coached speakers and comedians alike.

I worked on this process for over four years. What it taught me is that being funny is a very specific skill. Being funny with a group of people is a different skill than doing stand-up comedy. Likewise, doing stand-up comedy is different from delivering humor in a speech or presentation. During this time, I made mistakes and experienced major obstacles. I've learned the value of having a good teacher, coach, and mentor. Investing thousands of dollars in this process was worth it because I worked with someone who could really help me shortcut the process. Excellent coaches say the right thing at the right time. Jerry told me I was one of the few who had what it took to be good.

"Do you know how I know?" he asked me. "Because you're willing to do the work. Most of the people I work with aren't willing to do the work."

With Jerry, I experienced the difference between a subject matter expert and a substance matter expert. I first heard about the distinction between subject matter and substance matter experts from Tony Blauer, a self-defense expert. I bet you didn't see that one coming did you? Self-defense expert in a book on being funny? Absolutely! Some audiences can be mean. Tony stresses the difference between someone who knows their subject and someone who understands the substance that underlies the subject. A substance matter expert does more than just repeat fluff advice. Finally, I learned to do the work. I didn't always enjoy it. The jokes don't just come to me without effort; writing a joke is literally work. I had to set goals and work up to writing more and more jokes over time. Once I wrote Jerry and told him, "I've made a goal of writing 10 jokes a day." Then I asked, "How do I do it? Should I write one joke for 10 different headlines or 10 jokes on a single headline?"

"You're a rock star, Rick!" He said I should find a news headline that interested me and stick with the one headline and write 10 jokes. He closed with, "I can't wait to see what you come up with!"

At that point, I had to do the work on my own—just me and a blank piece of paper. Which is exactly how I started this chapter: just my notebook and me. But this time, I had an actual process for writing jokes, so I wouldn't be looking at a blank page for very long. Now, I have several processes for writing humor, consisting of different tools, techniques, and formulas that I've honed over the years. I also have Jerry's encouraging words in my head, along with the words from many other expert humorists, including John Vorhaus, Gene Perret, and Mel Helitzer.

As you continue reading, my hope is that you'll be encouraged and educated about the power of humor and how to make it work for you. Pay no attention to how funny you think you are (or aren't) now; it doesn't matter. I've lived what I'm sharing about in this book. I know that, if you do the work and put in the practice, you can become as funny as you'd like to become. And, please, let me and others know how this book helps you become a funnier you.

Next, when I wanted to transition from stand-up to humorous speaking and corporate comedy, I joined Toastmasters and was pleased to discover they had a humorous speech contest. I entered two years in a row and failed to advance to the final round. Oh, I was funny, but all of the laughter came at the expense of the greater purpose of the speech. I decided I needed a new approach. One last time, I attempted to advance to the final round and win the District 3 Humorous Speech contest. The third time, as they say, was the charm. With my new strategy, I won the competition.

I'm going to share what I learned—and more—with you.

2.

The 5 Obstacles to Using Humor and Being Funny

When it comes to being funny, adding humor to a speech or presentation and getting laughs puts you up against five major obstacles: mindset, willingness to practice, "vagueralities," no mentor, and no process.

The first two obstacles—mindset and a willingness to practice—are opposite sides of the same coin. Daniel Coyle explains the obstacles perfectly in his blog: "[A]dult prodigies succeed because they're able to work past two fundamental barriers: 1) the wall of belief that they can't do it; and 2) the grid of adult routines that keep them from spending time working intensively to improve skills. In other words, it's not so much about your 'natural talents,' as it is about your mindset and your habits."[11] Coyle's "wall of belief" is what I mean by your mindset and the "grid of adult routines" is what I mean by your willingness to practice.

The First Obstacle—Mindset

In my experience, the biggest obstacle you'll face is your own mindset because you'll question whether it's really possible to learn how to be funny, especially if you're trying to learn to be humorous later in life. In the May 2013 issue of *New Scientist*, David Robin says, "A decade ago, few neuroscientists would have agreed that adults can rival the learning talents of children. But we needn't be so defeatist. The mature brain, it turns out, is more supple than anyone thought.... Whatever you want to learn, it's never too late to charge those grey cells."[12]

Thanks to Professor Carol Dweck's research, we know that being funny results from both nature and nurture. In her book, *Mindset: The New Psychology of Success*, Dweck discusses achievement and success, demonstrating that now, more than ever, we know that our ability to do anything, including be humorous, is directly tied to our mindset.

Allow me to introduce you to the two mindsets I've observed as I've been teaching people about humor. First, when I've been networking or having dinner with other speakers, they often say to me, "I'd like to, but I'm just not funny." I usually smirk a little (mostly to myself, I hope) and say, "That's funny." This is what is call a "fixed mindset," believing that certain skills or personal attributes are either part of who you are, or they're not. Very often this first mindset comes with the fear of not wanting to look bad or fail. People with a fixed mindset prefer to tell themselves, "I'm just not _____." In this case, fill in the blank with "funny."

I witnessed this fixed and fearful mindset firsthand as I got started in stand-up comedy. During my beginning humor class, I met Jim, a very funny guy who made me laugh. But when the time came for our first performance on stage, Jim didn't get the laughs he wanted; he didn't do as well as he thought he should. The very next class, Jim had a breakdown: "I guess I'm not as funny as I thought." He tried one more class and one more performance. I thought it went well, considering it was only our second time on stage. Jim didn't think so, and he never came back to class. Based on just his first two beginning performances, Jim abandoned his quest to do stand-up comedy. I miss Jim. Don't be like Jim.

The second mindset is a "growth mindset," which is when

we believe that personal attributes like humor can be cultivated and grown through experience and practice. Jim and I started our stand-up comedy careers at the same time. Jim decided he "just wasn't as funny as he thought." In contrast, I decided I was as funny as ever, but I also learned that stand-up comedy was a different skill set than being naturally funny. I just needed more time to learn, experience, and grow into being a stand-up comic. And I was right. Even though I struggled, I didn't give up. Eventually, I found a comedy coach who could explain key details to me like the triggers of human laughter. With that valuable information and his coaching, I got my first paid gig just two months later and my first paid headlining gig three years after that. Before you get dollar signs in your eyes, you should know the gig only paid $25. I spent more that night on drinks at the club. Sssh, don't tell my wife.

Although I know I have a growth mindset, I still struggled and I also nearly gave up until I found a great coach. Even though my coach taught me excellent information and key details about being a good stand-up comic that had me excel in the long run, I still had to work hard, look bad, and experience off nights when my jokes fell flat or I got lukewarm laughs. That's why I have to tell you, even if you have a growth mindset, the second major obstacle to being funny is having access to quality information about comedy and then being committed to do the work to put that information into practice.

The Second Obstacle—Being Willing to Practice and Do the Work

The flip side of the mindset coin is the requirement to practice and do the work. The unfortunate truth about being funny is it requires practice, which means you'll try and fail and potentially look like a fool. None of us like failing or looking like a fool, especially, I think, when it comes to being funny. There's nothing worse than standing on a stage telling jokes and no one laughs. There is one thing worse actually and that's half-hearted, courtesy laughs. Those really hurt. It's easier not to try than to fail.

> *In other words, it is practice, not talent, that holds the key to success.*
> **Matthew Syed**

Regardless of whether you're a fan of the *Dilbert* cartoon or not, if you want to be funnier, you should become a fan of Scott Adams and his book, *How to Fail at Almost Everything and Still Win Big: Kind of the Story of My Life*. Adams is candid and very clear about the work required to be funny: "I'm better than 99 percent of the world (at ping-pong, Scrabble, and tennis) ... because I put in more practice than 99 percent of the world. There's no magic to it. I have a realistic understanding of how many hours it takes to be good at something. That keeps me from bailing out of things too soon."[13]

Bailing out too soon is easy to do. I nearly did it out of frustration. Most stand-up comics bail out because they're consistently confronted with the trial and error of not being good (i.e., failing). They just can't get enthusiastic about being bad, something Daniel Coyle, author of the *Talent Code*, encourages us to be, if we want to be good at anything: "To get good, it's helpful to be willing, or even enthusiastic, about being bad. Baby steps are the royal road to skill."[14]

Finally, if you really embrace the growth mindset, you

understand that effort is required for success and that ability lies on the other side of effort: "Those with a fixed mindset believe that effort is for people who don't have the ability to do something. People with a growth mindset admire effort. No matter what your ability is, effort is what ignites that ability and turns it into accomplishment."[15]

The first two obstacles I've discussed—mindset and practice—are within your control. The next three obstacles present a greater challenge because you can't necessarily control *them*.

> *Failing is often the best way to learn, and because of that, early failure is a kind of necessary investment.*
> **Chip Heath**

The Third Obstacle—Beware the Vaguralities

What is a "vaguerality"? Well, I made up the word by making a porte manteau, blending "vague" and "generality." When I decided to try stand-up comedy, even though I'd been told all my life I was funny, I was still bad at being an actual paid comedian. My naturally funny self didn't translate well to being alone on the stage. As a result, I took classes, read books, and I did research. My first stand-up comedy coach told me to try "writing from more emotion." He couldn't really teach me out to do that, but his vague, general instruction sent me on a journey to find someone who could *really* coach me. During my search, I found more of the same type of coaching and instruction, which just increased my frustration. Just like my first coach's advice to write with more emotion, other coaches also gave me more useless, vague generalities (vague + generality =

vagueralities) that I couldn't actually figure out how to put into action and use on stage. As you seek to learn how to add humor to your speeches, you, too, will probably encounter vagueralities like, "Tell humorous stories or anecdotes rather than jokes." But I didn't know how to write a humorous story, and no one was teaching me how. They were just telling me I should do it. Here is another piece of practically useless advice: "Know what makes *you* laugh." Even if I could identify what made me laugh, I couldn't explain why, so I couldn't recreate a similar type of joke to make others laugh.

And then there is one of my all-time favorite vagueralities: "Don't add humor to your speech. Uncover it." Excuse me? How does that *really* help me add more laughs to my speeches? My answer to vague, general advice about comedy is to create clarity by teaching would-be comedians a term often used in stand-up comedy: "laugh point." In your speech or presentation, a laugh point is simply where your audience laughs because you tell a joke, a funny story, or a humorous anecdote. It doesn't matter which you tell; it's the laugh that counts.

With a lot of effort, practice, and money spent over three years, I finally learned that humor is not a mystical trait reserved for a select few. I also learned it's possible to know how to create a humorous story and how to avoid offending your audience. And knowing your audience is part of being funny without being offensive, but it's just the beginning of the specific advice I teach other people about humor. Vagueralities are a pet peeve of mine and can quickly send me into a rant. Therefore, if something I present in this book strikes you as being vague and general, let me know. Just be nice about it because I have a bit of a fragile ego.

The Fourth Obstacle—No Access to a Great Teacher, Coach, or Mentor

The only way I cut through the vague, fluff advice I encountered too often on my journey to become a stand-up comic was by finally finding a great coach and teacher who offered me great actionable instruction. If you're looking for a good coach yourself, find someone who doesn't just repeat the typical advice you might have read in books or online but actually gives you clear instruction and steps you can take to be *funny*.

> The mediocre teacher tells. The good teacher explains. The superior teacher demonstrates. The great teacher inspires.
> **William Arthur Ward**

In Dan Gheesling's blog, "Why You Need a Mentor," Gheesling writes about the value of mentors: "For every goal I have achieved in my life, I can trace back each goal to a mentor or individual who helped achieve it.... Whatever it is that you want to accomplish in life, a mentor is going to kick start you on the path to achieve it."[16]

This need for mentoring was definitely true in my quest to become great at stand-up comedy and now, also, in my quest to become a professional paid speaker. I've experienced the value of a great coach and teacher versus a mediocre one.

> The average teacher explains complexity; the gifted teacher reveals simplicity.
> **Robert Brault**

A great coach will provide you information, drills, motivation, and inspiration to promote positive, powerful changes in your performance. Useful feedback is essential to improving. One of the greatest coaching skills is knowing how to amplify the effects of both feedback and practice on. In his blog, Daniel Coyle's offers two valuable rules for identifying great teachers and support:

Rule 9: Find the best teacher you can afford. One of the advantages of being an adult is that, unlike a kid, you can choose your own teacher. This is not a small thing. Find someone you like, and who maybe scares you a little (that is often a good sign).

Rule 10: Seek a training group. No matter what skill you're trying to build, you are more motivated when you are part of a tribe working toward a goal.[17]

The Fifth Obstacle—Techniques and Tools but No Applicable Process

Once you find a teacher or coach, the obstacle you may face is finding someone who can do two things: (1) teach you the techniques and tools to generate laughs and (2) teach you how to implement those techniques using a clear process.

Let me give you an example. When I first studied comedy writing and stand-up comedy, my teachers mainly focused on the joke—writing jokes and then assembling them into a bit or a set. As a result, I learned wonderful techniques for writing jokes and getting laughs, but I learned these techniques in isolation. I did not yet have the process where I try the jokes out on an audience and then revise and hone my jokes. In my experience, merely using techniques, tools, and secrets about how to write a joke just don't cut it. Like football, there's a time to do drills, and there's a time to scrimmage. During a scrimmage, you get to put all the drill work into practice. Wow, look at that, first a self-defense reference and now a football reference. What kind of crazy book is this? I'm out of control!

Comedy requires the same approach as football. Sometimes you will find usable information in books or on websites about how to get laughs. Or maybe you'll purchase a course from an expert that teaches you how to add humor to a speech or presentation. All these resources are good. From my personal experience, however, even if the course delivers on its promise of "secrets," you will still probably be left wondering how to integrate these tools and tips into an orderly process. The shotgun approach to tools and techniques will only increase your frustration and confusion. For example, using the rule of three is a common recommendation for adding humor to a speech. To use the rule of three, you set up a pattern and then break the pattern to create a surprise and therefore get a laugh. In a guest post on Patricia Fripp's blog, Darren LaCroix shares an example: "I'm excited to be visiting Sarasota. My friends were delighted to show me the local wildlife. They took me to see the dolphins at Miaka, the alligators at Sonata Island, and the drivers on Route 41."[18]

The rule of three is a fantastic laugh generator. But how do you use it in your speech? Understanding the tool or technique and how it works is just the beginning. The next step is having a process that guides, directs, and reveals opportunities to use the tool in your speech or presentation is the next level. In my experience, it's a missing link in comedy and humor training. As a result, *Hook 'em with Humor* focuses on processes. In this book, I focus on humor-generating processes, which are made up of tools. By concentrating on these learning methods, you can add tools as you encounter them because you'll understand the foundational techniques for using the tools.

Those are the five major obstacles you are going to encounter on the road to a funnier you. You can control the first two obstacles: mindset and practice. The remaining three—vagueralities, no coach/teacher, and no process—are obstacles you'll likely encounter once you overcome the first two. My goal with this book and my website, AFunnierYou.com, is to remove all five obstacles for you so you can become a funnier you.

3.

Humor Demystified

Regardless of your current beliefs about having a sense of humor and being funny, the ability to make people laugh is a skill. How do I know it's a skill? Simple. Here's the simple definition of "skill" from merriam-webster.com: "the ability to do something that comes from training, experience, or practice." Thankfully we live in a time when nearly everything has been studied or is being studied. One area of study that fascinates me is talent and skill.

> *Knowledge is not skill. Knowledge plus ten thousand times is skill.*
> **Shinichi Suzuki**

As a result of studying talent and skill acquisition, I'm convinced that EVERYTHING is a skill in that you can acquire it via training and practice. The vital ingredient then is knowing what to practice.

> *I wasn't naturally gifted in terms of size and speed; everything I did in hockey I worked for.*
> **Wayne Gretzky**

But What Should You Practice?

One of the keys to excelling at an activity or skill is to break it down into subskills so that it can be reasonably learned and mastered. Any advice about becoming good at anything, including being funny, will not be helpful if it's too broad and general. In *The 4-Hour Chef* and in his numerous articles and videos, Tim Ferriss discusses rapid skill acquisition. He specifically recommends deconstructing a skill and breaking it down and then focusing on the most valuable pieces, focusing most of your attention on the 20% that provides the 80% return. When it comes to creating laughter, one theory stands apart from the rest and that is the theory of SURPRISE.

> *Everything should be made as simple as possible, but not simpler.*
> **Albert Einstein**

Why Do People Laugh?

People laugh for a variety of reasons and humor has been studied for centuries. Theories are fine and maybe a little interesting but if we are interested in making people laugh we need to focus, as Tim Ferriss recommends, on the 20% that provides the 80% return.[19] Surprise is our primary focus for a couple of reasons:

> *All the great speakers were bad speakers at first.*
> **Ralph Waldo Emerson**

1. Mel Helitzer says surprise is a necessary element of humor. So, it's not just a theory, it's crucial.
2. In *The Ten Commandments of Comedy*, Gene Perret boldly proclaims, "Surprise is such an essential element of comedy that if your joke, story, anecdote, or piece of business doesn't have a twist or a surprise to it, it's not comedy."

And surprise happens to have a mechanical component that allows anyone who understands it to use that mechanism to make people laugh. How do we surprise people? We are going to surprise people and make them laugh by setting up (or recognizing) an assumption or expectation and then crushing that expectation or assumption. Thankfully, we can create surprise by using our audience's human nature against them. In their book, *Understanding Interpersonal Communication: Making Choices in Changing Times*, Richard West and Lynn H. Turner discuss something called the "listening gap." No, the listening gap is not the term for when husbands appear to be listening to their wives but aren't really listening. No, the term for that is "being impolite" and I promise I'm working on it.

Back to the listening gap, basically, human beings can understand up to 800 words a minute, but most people speak in the 150 to 200 words a minute range.[22] As a result, your audience is always listening ahead of you as the speaker. They're creating a visual as you speak, even anticipating or expecting what you're going to say next. It's human nature. No one can avoid it. In addition, the words and phrases we use all have an expected and assumed meaning behind them. Likewise, our tone and body language add to that anticipated meaning.

As a result of the "listening gap" and assumed meaning of words, you can play with people's visualizing and assumed meaning making to "surprise" them when your words don't match what they thought you would say. For example, if I asked you, "Do you ever wake up grumpy?" what am I asking you? It's not a trick question. I'm asking you, "Do you ever wake up in a bad mood?" At least that's the assumed meaning under my first question, and that apparent meaning carries with it a natural response. What if we twist the assumed meaning? What if we know that our question is "Do you ever wake up Grumpy?" then our answer can be, "No, I just let him sleep." We would get a laugh. Why? Because we twisted the assumed meaning and created a surprise. The key skill to creating a surprise and generating a laugh is to identify these assumed meanings and expectations.

Review

Although there are a lot of ways to make people laugh, one of the primary theories of producing laughter is surprise. Surprise is so powerful that some humor experts believe surprise is present 90% of the time when people laugh. Therefore, to begin learning to be funny or funnier, we're going to focus on surprise. How do we surprise people? As it relates to speaking, we surprise our audience and generate a laugh by first recognizing the expectation or assumption, we are creating in the mind of our audience. A major ally will be recognizing stories and words with double meanings. Once the audience has a clear picture (expectation), we are going to surprise them by changing the meaning. As a result, the primary subskill of using surprise to create laughter is to recognize what people will assume or expect from what you say. The second subskill is to twist the assumed meaning to something unexpected.

Time to Practice

Brian Kiley, a comedian, started a joke in this way, "The other day our boy talked back to my wife. She told him to do something, and he said, "No. I don't want to." So I had to pull him aside and say, "Listen, you have to...."

Up until this point, what is the assumption or what is the expected, acceptable way for Brian to complete his sentence? Form the answer in your mind. Got it? Now that you've identified the expected conclusion in your mind, you're primed for Brian Kiley's twist.

> The other day our boy talked back to my wife. She told him to do something, and he said, "No. I don't want to." So I had to pull him aside and say, "Listen, you have to ... teach me how to do that!"

A note about timing: the three dots, an ellipsis, is often used in writing comedy to indicate a pause, allowing audience members time to solidify the assumption and expectation in their mind prior to you twisting it for the laugh. See? Timing can be taught—and learned, too! Your first task is simply to recognize the expectation or assumption carried with the statement. Let's practice. I'm going to give you the set-up from four jokes without the twist they put at the end. Identify the assumptions or expectations in the set-up statement before reading further to see how the comedian twisted expectations:

Set-up Statement: A man walks into a bar.
Assumption:_____
Set-up Statement: Women are crazy; take my wife.
Assumption:_____
Set-up Statement: I just flew in from Chicago.
Assumption:_____

Set-up Statement: I saw a billboard that says 1 in 4 people in America struggle with hunger.
Assumption:_____

Okay, now you've practiced identifying the expected assumptions. Now let's see how the comedians gave their audiences a surprise twist.

Set-up Statement: A man walks into a bar.
Humorous Twist: A man walks into a bar. Ouch!
Set-up Statement: Women are crazy; take my wife.
Humorous Twist: Women are crazy; take my wife. Please!
Set-up Statement: I just flew in from Chicago.
Humorous Twist: I just flew in from Chicago and, boy, are my arms tired.
Set-up Statement: I saw a billboard that says 1 in 4 people in America struggle with hunger.
Humorous Twist: I saw a billboard that says 1 in 4 people in America struggle with hunger. I don't know how they do it. I give right in.

The idea is to twist the statement's expected meaning until the statement has an entirely new meaning.

Example: A man walks into a bar. Ouch!

The expectation or assumption is that we will hear a story about a man in a bar.

How can we defeat or twist the expectation? Simply add the word "ouch," and we have twisted on WHY a man walks into a bar (to get a drink) to now mean that he literally walked into a bar.

Using the literal meaning is a common way to twist a statement.

Examples: "I just flew in from Chicago and, boy, are my arms tired."

"Call me a cab." "Ok, you're a cab."

Another fun way to twist a statement is to use exaggeration.

Example: Brian Kiley: "My wife is the one who talked me into shaving my head; she said I'd look much younger and I do. I now look like I'm a week old."

We can also twist on the double meanings of words.

Rodney Dangerfield: "What a childhood I had. Once on my birthday my ol' man gave me a bat. The first day I played with it, it flew away."

We can twist with an afterthought:

Rick Olson: "My wife and I were about to embark on this bicycle ride with 8,000 other cyclists.... That is a lot of spandex."

We can twist with the downside or negative spin:

Rick Olson: "I am grateful for the good in my life.... I just wish it didn't cost so much."

We can twist with the upside or positive spin:

"In Pasadena, three bears broke a door to a residence and were seen frolicking in a backyard pool. Thankfully no one was injured since Goldilocks wasn't home."

We can twist by clarifying the meaning:

Jim Gaffigan: "Babies are a lot of work, I try to pitch in, I do diapers. I don't change them. I just say 'You need to do this diaper.'"

Most statements carry with them certain expectations or assumptions. Those assumptions primarily center around the answers to questions beginning with *who, what, when, where, why,* or *how.*

Who: Jerry Corley

"You know what my baby loves to play with? Chest hair, and she'll yank on it too. Finally I had to say to my wife, 'You know, you might want to get that lasered.'"

What: Brian Kiley

"One thing I remember, we used to do something called

family night, where we set aside one night a week for each of us to spend a night with a different family."

When: Brian Kiley

"You want your kids to be perfect and they're not. My wife told me today that my daughter's been shoplifting and now I have to deal with that ... I'm going to wait until after my birthday."

Why: Jim Gaffigan

"We had all of our babies at home ... just to make you feel uncomfortable."

How: Brian Kiley

"I found out today that my wife's parents are coming to visit and my wife hasn't mentioned anything yet. I can just tell the way the animals in my neighborhood are behaving."

Set-up Statement: When I cook, I use wine.

Assumption/Expectations(s):_____

Now write 10 possible humor lines that could follow this set-up statement:

1. Sometimes I even put it in the food.

2. _____

3. _____

4. _____

5. _____

6. _____

7. _____

8. _____

9. _____

10. _____

You might wonder, why 10? Simple. Sometimes you'll quit too early and miss out on the best joke. Writing jokes is a bit like working out. If you quit too soon you miss out on the biggest benefit. But, on the other hand, writing jokes is nothing like going to the gym because jokes make me laugh and the gym makes me cry.

You will find out that one of the common mistakes is giving up too soon, and part of the solution is developing the habit that Gene Perret calls overwriting. Also, when people start a creative act, they tend to be "in their heads" thinking too much. Spending a little more time in the act of creation allows the process to gain momentum. Furthermore, if you remove the burden of being good and first go for quantity rather than quality, you'll have more fun and be more likely to enjoy the process. Finally, write 10 humorous lines because John Vorhaus says so!

In *The Comic Toolbox*, John Vorhaus described the Rule of Nine in the following way:

> For every ten jokes you tell, nine will be trash. For every ten ideas you have, nine won't work. For every ten times you risk, you fail.
>
> Depressing? Not really. In fact, the rule of nine turns out to be highly liberating because once you embrace it, you instantly and permanently lose the toxic expectation of succeeding every time.[23]

You now know the biggest obstacles you're going to face, and that humor is not some mystical trait available to a select few. No! Humor is available to every person and every speaker who is willing to study and practice the skills and subskills of making people laugh. The next big question is, how do you add humor to your speeches and presentations? You're now ready for The Laugh Generator Process.

4.

The Laugh Generator™ Process

How it all began...

As I sat there waiting for the contest results, I couldn't help wishing it wouldn't be like the last time and the time before that. Please! Not second place again! Was I doomed to always finish second? In high school, I was voted the second funniest person in the class. Who does that? I soothed my ego by insisting I came in second place because I was the class wit and not the class clown. Some things even I wouldn't do for a laugh. While Chad ... Chad knew no boundaries.

And then there was that contest in college: "The Funniest Person on Campus."

Crap!

And finally, last year's humorous speech contest. I won second place at the division contest but didn't advance. Second place! Really? Still, everyone around me insists: "You're SOOOooooo Funny!" Whatever! I guess I'm just not funny enough.

What is taking them so long to get the results tallied? Alright, here we go, the results are final and they are about to reveal....

Third? Seriously? THIRD! What the...? I'm going backwards! DEVASTATING! I approach the stage to receive the award for ... third place. I guess I should have been more specific when I wished for something other than second place. Oh well, I guess I'm done. No sense in continuing to compete if I'm not going to win.

The next day, well-meaning friends sent their typical emails: "Rick made a valiant effort but was awarded 3rd place. I felt he should have finished at least 2nd, so I suspect the voting by the judges was very close." Another wrote, "Rick was definitely robbed. He was amazing as usual!" But one of my friend's emails stood out and got me thinking.... "In my opinion, Rick is at a bit of a disadvantage in this type of contest. He does stand-up comedy while Toastmaster judges are looking for stories."

For the previous two years, I had studied stand-up comedy, comedy writing, joke writing, and improv comedy. My friend's email made sense to me. I was approaching the Humorous Speech contest like I would a stand-up comedy set. And maybe that was the problem. It wasn't that I wasn't funny enough. I was using the wrong approach.

After getting paid for doing comedy, there I was at a Toastmaster's contest only able to get third place! I felt like I was starting from scratch all over again. Joining Toastmasters was supposed to help me transition to corporate speaking and becoming a professional—and humorous—motivational speaker. But, here I was trying to prove I can be the funniest person in the room, but it turns out I'm only the third funniest! Because it's my nature to figure out how things work, especially when I'm not achieving my professional goals, I started reading more books on humorous speaking, internet articles on adding humor to a speech, and watching YouTube videos filled with tips on being a funny speaker. And what I found was mostly ... fluff. Vague, general advice—vagueralities!

I kept reading this same fluff stuff advice about speaking humorously, hashed and rehashed over and over again across the internet: Use the Rule of Three, Use exaggeration, Don't tell jokes. And this one: make sure your humor has a purpose and a point. Which was a tad bit ironic because most of the humor tips I found didn't have a purpose or a point.

Oh, these fluff experts are well meaning—when they aren't trying to scare folks. "Don't use humor or tell jokes," they warn. "It's DANGEROUS!" Whatever!

And then I did what I should have done at the very beginning. I looked at the scoring criteria on the judge's ballot. By reviewing the actual criteria for winning, I set my creativity in motion resulting in a process that advanced me past the division contest to become the Toastmaster District 3 Humorous Speaking Champion. I now call my new technique The Laugh Generator Process. It violates all the advice and rules of the so-called experts. That's right, I *added* humor to my speech—instead of uncovering it. I told jokes, rather than humorous anecdotes. I didn't consider what might tickle my audience's funny bone or even what made *me* laugh. Most of that regurgitated advice was of no use. Instead, I combined techniques from speech writing, stand-up, and comedy writing, along with improv comedy. And...

My Process Worked!

The third time I competed in the Humorous Speech Contest, I won! My idea worked, the process worked, and ... I still wasn't satisfied.

Sure, it worked for me, but I was "naturally funny" and studied comedy so I needed to know if it would work for others. I spent a whole year refining and creating an elegant process that allows anyone, regardless of natural ability, to add humor to a speech or presentation. And now I'm sharing it with you. In response to sharing my process with my friend, Zeke, I received this email: "Thanks for your help. I was kind of shocked, but you were right. The guy who came in 2nd behind me was naturally funny and had way more laughs, but...."

I'll get to the "BUT" shortly.

Very cool, considering the email Zeke had sent me before: "Rick, I'm still thinking about what you said last weekend. How can you make me funny?" That weekend I told him that even though he didn't think he was funny and his wife didn't think he was funny, I could help him win the Humorous Speech Contest. And after two coaching sessions, I watched Zeke win the Division Humorous Speech contest, and he went on to compete on the district stage for his first time.

Now back to the "BUT." This is what he wrote in his second email: "... but ... he had no message to tie it together."

A very common piece of advice for speakers is to ensure the humor in your speech has a point and a purpose, so I took that advice in another direction. As part of my writing process, I decided to let the speech have the point and the purpose, and then use what I knew about generating laughs to provide laughs—laughs that didn't distract from the point and purpose of the speech but rather enhanced it. And that's the point of humor in a speech ... to enhance the content, to provide some "seasoning" that makes it more enjoyable.

The Laugh Generator™ Process

Mark Twain said, "Get your facts first, then you can distort them as you please."

I love this Mark Twain quote. It's become a mantra of sorts for me because the quote's simplicity is the very essence of creating a joke and getting a laugh. If you are ever struggling with the process, just think about Twain's quote.

Step 1: Give and Record the Speech

The first step in the process is to actually give your speech, tell your story, give your presentation, etc. Whatever you want to add humor to, you need to just "give it." Ideally, you will present to an audience (any audience), which is why I suggest you join Toastmasters™. If you don't have an audience, give your speech to your dog, cat, or goldfish. For simplicity, I'm going to use the word "speech," but realize "it" could be a story, an anecdote, a presentation, a lesson, a workshop, or any time you're in front of three or more people speaking. When you give your speech, record it.

Next, you are going to have the recording transcribed. I use a service called Rev.com and pay to have an exact transcription, which costs $1.25 for each recorded minute. The reason you need to actually give your speech is that you don't speak the way you write. Language for the eye (to be read) is different from language for the ear (to be heard). Your humor, just like your speech, needs to be designed for the ear. Throughout this book, I provide examples of funny lines. As you read them, they may not be funny at all because they're being read.

Humor to be delivered is different from humor to be read. Remember that. For the humor to have the best chance of working, you will want to create the twists using the spoken word and not the written word. If you used the written word, the flow and pacing will not work as well when you actually give your speech.

Next, you will receive a written transcription.

Step 2: Review and Analyze the Transcription

Go through the transcript and isolate each fact and every sentence. Then ask yourself these questions:
- What are the assumptions, implied meanings, or expected answer/response?
- What are the appropriate or expected reactions or responses?
- What is the literal meaning? Is there an upside/downside?
- Does something need to be clarified?
- Which words "jump" out as having double meanings?

Step 3: Twist the Meaning

Look for any opportunities to twist the meaning in any of these ways:
- The Literal Meaning
- Exaggeration
- Compare/Contrast
- Double Meaning Words (play on words, double entendre, pun on all or part)
- An Afterthought
- The Upside/Downside
- The need to clarify a meaning
- Answers to questions: who, what, when, where, why, and how

Step 4: Create Potential Laugh Lines

After you've identified expected meanings and assumptions, you will now create potential laugh lines. And just to make sure you have the best laugh possible, try to create 10 different laugh lines. Don't judge the laugh lines and don't judge yourself. Just allow the creative process to happen.

Step 5: Give Your New Speech

Now give your new speech a try on an actual audience. Record this second version of your speech, too, and have it transcribed. Then repeat the process so you can hone and refine what you've created until you have a completely new and improved, rock-solid speech with plenty of beneficial laughs.

This is The Laugh Generator Process. Here it is again as a quick summary:
- Give your speech and record it.
- Isolate each line and identify the expected meanings or assumptions.
- Review the checklist for opportunities of possible twists.
- Create 10 potential laugh lines.
- Give your speech again, record it, and transcribe it. Repeat.

The Process in Action

Let me show you two real life examples of how The Laugh Generator Process could have been used to get a speaker some laughs. The laugh was right there within the speech, and my process for generating laughs would have revealed it for the speaker.

Here is the first example:

A coaching client of mine, Xander, (not his real name) missed a perfect opportunity to get a laugh in a presentation when he was sharing the story of a boat trip, where he had to anchor his boat during a bad storm. During the story, Xander said, "I didn't want my boat to end up on the rocks." What does "on the rocks" also mean? It's a way to order a drink. If he had just taken a second to recognize the other meaning, Xander could have made the audience laugh by adding, "I didn't want my boat to end up on the rocks because ... boat on the rocks bad, scotch on the rocks good!" The audience would have laughed at the surprise of that phrase being twisted by capitalizing on its two meanings. Xander could have heightened the joke even more this way: "I didn't want my boat to end up on the rocks, so I did what any captain would do ... I went to the liquor cabinet. Because, boat on the rocks bad, scotch on the rocks good!"

Here's the second example:

Another speaker I evaluated, Crystal, shared a travel story about going through the security line at the airport. At one point she said, "My husband and kids were asked to go to one security line, and I was asked to go to a separate security line." At this point, if you've traveled lately, you understand extra security measures and searches. So you know the implied and expected meaning (or reaction, in this case) is one of anxiety by this woman about having to be searched. If she would have twisted the meaning, she might have said, "All I could think was ... Phew! Finally, some alone time." Her audience would have laughed. She might have heightened it even more by comparing and contrasting this way: "My husband and kids were asked to go to one security line, and I was asked to go to a separate security line. I looked at my husband, and he was freaking out, while all I could think was ... Finally! Some me time."

The Laugh Generator Process is the first tool in your

comedy toolkit. Humor starts with this process. And because it's a new way of thinking and a new way of creating a speech, getting good at the process will take some time. Please keep in mind that the very heart of the process is exactly what I shared in "Humor Demystified." Being funny is simply recognizing the assumption or expectation, twisting the meaning, and then shattering that expectation. The resulting "surprise" will generate laughter. The more you practice, the easier this process will become.

My goal has been to provide you with a complete guide to becoming a funnier you. After all, that's the name of my website: AFunnierYou.com. To accomplish that goal, in the Resources section of this book, you will find "What Now?" where I provide information about what and how to practice to become funnier faster. Plus, I provide you with a complete, 90-Day Humor Improvement Plan that you can follow, so the journey doesn't overwhelm you.

And because I know firsthand how valuable a coach and a group of like-minded people can be, I've provided opportunities for you to get support through private and group coaching. Find out more by visiting my website at AFunnierYou.com.

5.

The 7 Reasons Humor Is a Must or You Fail

I want to know something. Why are you getting up in front of an audience of anywhere from one to 100,000 people and daring to speak? What do you want?

Whatever the reason—whatever you want to achieve—depends on one thing and one thing only: how well your audience responds to you, your message, and your call to action. It all rests solely on your shoulders. Well, not your shoulders exactly, but it is your responsibility. Are you there for the audience? Do you have their best interest in mind? If so, keep reading. If not, move on. There's no future for you as a speaker, presenter, salesperson, preacher, or business owner if you don't care about your audience.

I've discovered something—a secret if you will—about your audience. They really *do* want to pay attention to you. The audience wants to listen to you. They want to remember what you're saying, and they want to focus on you. They don't want to be bored. Who would? Are you helping them? Are you investing in your speaking skills so you can give your very best to your audience?

Giving an effective, riveting presentation isn't just one skill; it's a toolbox of skills. Generating laughs is one of those skills. Jeffrey Gitomer, an author, speaker, and business trainer, says, "Some people look at it as a 'laugh'—I look at it as a learning device, listening tool, attention grabber, self-healer, powerful selling tool, and—of course—fun."[24] A laugh is all those things, but it's also something more. It's a gift—a gift you give your audience that provides enormous benefits for them and for you.

1. Laughter Benefits Your Audience

Stress reduction is one of laughter's biggest benefits. People are stressed. In fact, according to the American Institute of Stress, three out of four doctor visits are for stress-related illnesses, resulting in $300 billion worth of costs associated with medical bills and lost productivity every year.[25] According to The American Institute of Stress, NY, as shared by Statistic Brain Research Institute, 77 percent[26] of people regularly experience the following stress-related physical symptoms:

> I've learned that people will forget what you said, people will forget what you did, but people will never forget how you made them feel.
> Maya Angelou

Effects of Stress [27]

- Memory problems
- Inability to concentrate
- Poor judgment
- Seeing only the negative
- Anxious or racing thoughts
- Constant worrying
- Moodiness
- Irritability or short temper
- Agitation, inability to relax
- Feeling overwhelmed
- Sense of loneliness and isolation

- Depression or general unhappiness
- Aches and pains
- Procrastinating or neglecting responsibilities

In contrast, when people laugh, they get the following benefits:

Benefits of Laughter [28]

- Increased endorphins and dopamine
- Improved immune system[29]
- Increased relaxation response
- Reduced pain
- Reduced stress
- Increased creativity
- Improved problem-solving ability
- Enhanced memory
- Elevated mood and feelings of well-being
- Reduced depression, anxiety, and tension
- Increased self-esteem and resilience
- Increased hope, optimism, energy, and vigor

So the first benefit of laughter is how it helps your audience momentarily undo the stress of their day and their week, which is truly a gift.

Laughter is an instant vacation.
Milton Berle

2. Grab Your Audience's Attention

Your very first task as a speaker is to get your audience's attention. Failing to intentionally create interest and earn attention could mean disaster. According to Matt Abrams, a lecturer at Stanford, "Your job as a presenter is to engage your audience, to pull them forward in their seats. Unfortunately, audiences can be easily distracted, and they habituate quickly."[30] John Medina, author of *Brain Rules*, explains that "You've got 30 seconds before they start asking the question, 'Am I going to pay attention to you or not?' The instant you open your mouth, you are on the verge of having your audience check out."[31] Sam Horn agrees in *Got Your Attention?: How to Create Intrigue and Connect with Anyone*, saying, "Clearly, we have an impatience epidemic, and we're suffering from alienation and attention bankruptcy, all at the same time."[32]

In other words, if you can't get people's attention, you'll never get their connection.

If you've been on any commercial airline flight, as the flight attendant starts to give the requisite announcements, you'll notice very few people paying attention. There might be that rare individual flying for the first time, eyes wide with terror, intently fixated on how to survive a crash in water and wondering why everyone else isn't listening. Mostly, though, people aren't listening. They're sending a final text, reading a magazine, or hoping the passenger in the next seat will keep to themselves.

In contrast to run-of-the-mill announcements, you may have heard flight attendants, like Marty Cobb use humor like this (viewed over 22 million times on YouTube) to grab people's attention so they will listen to the announcements: "If I could pretend to have your attention for just a few moments...

my ex-husband, my new boyfriend, and their divorce attorney are going to show you the safety features of this 737, 800 series. It's been a long day for me.... Position your seatbelt tight and low across your hips like my grandmother wears her support bra."[33] Everyone watches, listens, and pays attention to this announcement. Humor breaks through boredom or distractions, letting your audience know what you say will be worth their time.

James Altucher's number one method for being a great speaker is to start off with a joke. He says, "People need to laugh within the first 30 seconds or else you're going back to your cubicle at the pencil factory and they will never remember you." Altucher spends a couple of hours writing that first joke, making sure it's relevant to the audience he's addressing.[34] But starting with a joke to earn the audience's attention certainly isn't new. In *Successful Persuasion Through Public Speaking*, John Hayes interviews Zig Ziglar who attributes his success as a speaker to telling a joke right away: "My first objective is to have them laughing within the first 30 seconds."[35] Did you notice how these recommendations all mentioned 30 seconds? I don't think it's a coincidence that James Altucher, Zig Ziglar, and John Medina all focused on this short amount of time.

3. Keep Your Audience's Attention and Ensure They Are Listening

Your first goal is to grab your audience's attention. Your second goal is to keep it. Medina's research on the brain demonstrates that people don't pay attention to boring things: "You've got seconds to grab someone's attention and only 10 minutes to keep it. At 9 minutes and 59 seconds, you must do something to regain attention and restart the clock." Making your audience laugh is certainly a great way to restart that clock. As one of the most recognized speakers, Ziglar uses humor for this very purpose. In fact, he says he does "everything humanly possible to hold your attention," and he reliably tells a joke every 7 to 9 minutes. "And every time I do," says Ziglar, "you know what happens? I see 50 or 100 people in the audience turn to somebody and say 'what did he say?'"

Jeffrey Gitomer emphasizes the need for laughter and humor in a presentation because it's tied to people's memory: "Whatever you say AFTER you say something funny will be heard and remembered 10 times more....In short, laughter leads to listening and creates the highest listening environment."[36]

4. Help your Audience Remember and Learn

Your third goal is helping your audience remember. Author and speaker Lilly Walters says, "The success of your presentation will be judged not by the knowledge you send but by what the listener receives." Research suggests that humor produces psychological and physiological benefits that help students learn.[37] The benefits to learning are not just found in youthful audiences but in those that may deal with age-related memory loss.[38] In case you didn't know, memory is the third thing "to go." Don't bother asking what the first two are, I don't remember. The reason laughter facilitates learning has to do with what happens in the brain when we laugh. One theory shows how laughter improves learning because it engages both sides of the brain.[39] Laughter also causes brain cells to release dopamine, and dopamine acts like a "save" button.[40] I wonder which button is the "undo" button.

5. Encourage a Willing Mindset in Your Audience

So laughter helps you grab attention, keep attention, and improves the likelihood your message will be remembered. But laughter's benefits don't stop there. Learning is just the beginning when it comes to dopamine. Dopamine's impact on the body is felt in many different areas,[41] including "motivation, memory, behavior and cognition, attention, sleep, mood, learning, and, oh yeah, pleasurable reward."[42] Notice two keywords in that list: *mood* and *motivation*. As your audience is laughing, their stress is being relieved and counteracted, their fear is being disengaged,[43] they're listening, learning, and finally, their mood is enhanced and their motivation primed. When you have your audience laughing, you have their attention. You know they're listening. Every laugh is priming their brains to hear, think about your message, and consider your call to action because, at a subtle level, you're helping your audience know, like, and trust you—the key to winning over people's hearts and minds.

6. Help Your Audience Know, Like, and Trust You

According to Bob Burg's well-known Golden Rule of Networking,[44] "All things being equal, people will do business with, and refer business to, those people they know, like and trust." So what can you as a speaker or presenter do to ensure that connection with your audience? You already know the answer.

> *When you get an audience laughing, you've got them on your side.*
> **Mohammed Qahtani**

Nothing builds rapport faster than humor.[45] Jeffrey Gitomer says that without humor, an invisible barrier exists between getting to know someone on the surface and getting to know someone on a deeper level.[46]

According to Sophie Scott, a British neuroscientist who conducts research on the neuroscience of voices, speech, and laughter, says laughter is the strongest bond builder there is between humans. "It's a behavior we think is about amusement," she explains, "but actually it's about affiliation, agreement and affection."[47] Isn't that a perfect alliteration? Almost tickles my ears. She also says this "bond building" will not only make you more likeable, but "encourages others to root for you and desire your success."[48] In fact, humor is so powerful at building trust, one study proved that the use of humor in negotiations resulted in a 15% improved return and increased satisfaction on both sides.[49] *Reader's Digest* was surprised to learn that tweeting didn't improve trust but being an expert who makes people laugh does.[50]

Finally, we know humor and trust go together, which is no surprise to me. Research shows that effective humor creates "psychological safety," a key element to building trust between people.[51]

7. How Making Your Audience Laugh Benefits You

The benefits of laughter will return to you ten, fifty, or a hundredfold, depending on the size of the audience. One of the most remarkable discoveries in neuroscience is a specific category of neurons called mirror neurons. In 1992, a team at the University of Parma, Italy discovered "mirror neurons." Marco Iacoboni pioneered the research on mirror neurons or the "smart cells" in our brain that allow us to understand others.

In a *Scientific American* interview, he said,

> We use our body to communicate our intentions and our feelings. The gestures, facial expressions, body postures we make are social signals, ways of communicating with one another. Mirror neurons are the only brain cells we know of that seem specialized to code the actions of other people and also our own actions.[52]

These neurons are widely dispersed throughout your brain and activate to mimic what another being does. You could consider them a neural Wi-Fi,[53] which instantly creates shared experience. Mirror neurons connect us to other humans. Remember the shortest distance between two people according to Victor Borge? Laughter!

Smiling and laughing are so important to us as humans that our brains contain mirror neurons specifically for detecting smiles and laughter.[53] This means then that when you make your audience laugh, their laughter causes your mirror neurons to fire, resulting in you receiving the very benefits described above.

Plus, you're speaking for a reason, correct? Whatever that reason, whatever action you hope your audience will take, with humor, your call to action has a better chance of evoking action. Your audience is listening and every individual mind has been primed. Conditions are perfect.

Laughter is the shortest distance between two people.
Victor Borge

And who knows...?

The first action they take may just be to give you a standing ovation. I'm being serious. When Sean Stephenson, a renowned speaker, was asked the secret to getting a standing ovation, he said, "You must make a person laugh hard, cry, and rethink their life. People are stressed. If you can create a speech that makes people laugh, that will relieve their stress, even momentarily."[54]

A Bonus Reason to Use Humor—Event Organizers Want It

As a speaker, are you interested in more gigs, more speaking engagements, more referrals, and ultimately, more revenue? Humor is a key ingredient to obtain that which you desire. The reason is simple, says Grant Baldwin, a professional speaker, "Your best marketing tool is a great talk."[55] In *Speaking for Success*, Bob "Idea Man" Hooey says, in response to the question, "*Do you have to be funny?*," "Only if you want to be paid!"[56] Alan Weiss further clarifies how humor improves your odds at get speaking gigs in *Million Dollar Speaking: The Professional's Guide to Building Your Platform*. He says, "Meeting planners love to evaluate potential speakers by viewing demo tapes for a few minutes, making visceral decisions based on such ephemera as a funny story, stage movement, and appearance."[57] Brian Lord, speaker agent and vice president of Premiere Speakers Bureau, says he'd heard experts claim that event planners and corporate audiences really wanted content. But he observed that in reality, "When it came time to book a speaker, the speakers that used a lot of humor and stories—those were the ones that kept getting booked."[58]

Jeremy Poincenot, inspirational speaker and coach, reinforces the importance of humor, if you want to make money at speaking: "You too might have a really inspiring story and lots of useful lessons, but if the audience isn't entertained, you'll most likely not get booked. Some people say you don't have to be funny to be a speaker. I agree, but I think you have to be funny to be a *paid* speaker."[59]

Steve Gilliland, speaker and author of *40 Irrefutable Steps to Building a Substantial Speaking Business*, says since he began his speaking career in 1999, his goal was to create memorable presentations and become a world-class speaker. "I want my presentation to be extremely entertaining and funny," says Gilliland, "but impossible to replicate because of the emotional content that would resonate and emotionally connect with members of my audiences."[60]

Hearing about the importance of your talk and having an entertaining speech is one thing, but are there really more opportunities for humorous presenters to speak? A sample of the speaking opportunities posted on SpeakerMatch.com, a website for emerging and aspiring speakers of which I am a member, shows how much people value humor and how often humor is mentioned and considered "a plus":

- Organizer is looking for up to 2 motivational speakers to address STEM franchise owners coming in for a convention from all over the country. Marketing, education, and business experience is welcome. Franchise promotes STEM education for 4-14 year olds. A sense of humor a big plus!
- Organizer is looking for a motivational speaker to help kick off a week of training for a staff of 80 professional and non-professional education service providers. The speaker will have 1 hour. Audience ages range from mid-20s to 70s. Humor is a plus.

- Organizer is looking for a Keynote speaker to provide a motivational and funny presentation that can relate to the sales profession for a group of 25 sales professionals.
- Organizer is looking for a humorous, motivational, anti-bullying speaker for middle school aged students.
- Organizer is looking for a speaker to help motivate staff as they grow and develop into a global market. A sense of humor and creativity is appreciated.
- Organizer is looking for a 60 to 90 minute humorous motivational speaker to present at a medical staff conference with a group of 100.
- Organizer is looking for a humorous motivational speaker for a 1 hour presentation. Ideal topic is team building and stress management.

This trend for more entertainment isn't going away. Imagine the booking possibilities if, in addition to your other high-content programs, you offered a version that included high entertainment and high engagement.

6.

The Simple Joke Writing System™

Writing jokes is one way to quickly add more laughs to your speeches and presentations. After you've added laugh points (jokes) using The Laugh Generator, the next step is to actually write jokes about the content of your speech or presentation. Please note though, if you are happy with the number of laughs in your speech, you don't need to take this step. If, however, you want to explore more joke possibilities, the Simple Joke Writing System will do that for you.

Again, the Internet is filled with advice warning you against telling jokes and urging you to make sure your humor stays on topic. But that's where the typical advice ends. The "experts" never really tell you how to create jokes, let alone how to create them so they don't divert your audience's attention. So what's the best way to create jokes (laugh points) that aren't a diversion? Use the content of your speech or stories as the starting point to write jokes, that's how.

Remember this example of a missed opportunity to add a laugh?

Statement: Airport security asked my kids and husband to go to one line, and they asked me to go to another line.

The expected emotional response is one of fear or trepidation, but we can twist that expectation and use an unexpected emotional response to get a laugh.

Humorous Statement: Airport security asked my kids and husband to go to one line, and they asked me to go to another line. All I thought was "Finally! Some me time."

In that same speech, the speaker said, "I noticed that standing in line at airport security was a lot like being in line at Disneyland." That line got some chuckles from the audience, but there's also a missed opportunity to get even bigger laughs.

Combining Ideas to Get Even Bigger Laughs

In *The New Comedy Writing Step by Step*, Gene Perret says most comedy is a combination of two or more ideas.[61] So let's combine the ideas of Disneyland and Airport Security and see what jokes we can create. The first step is to list everything you can think of for both ideas: Disneyland and airport security. Important note: during this process, DO NOT edit or censor yourself. Just let the ideas happen and your creativity roll. You'll have time to edit later. If you edit now, you'll shut down your creativity (no joke) and not find the gem of the joke.

Step 1: Isolate the Line

This is similar to the Speech Laugh Generator Process.

I noticed that standing in line at airport security was a lot like being in line at Disneyland.

Step 2: Generate an Association List for 2 or 3 Primary Subject Areas

Let's do this exercise now. Take out a piece of paper and draw a line down the middle. On one side write "Disneyland" and on the other side write "Airport or Airport Security." Now, start writing everything you can think of related to "Disneyland" in the left column and everything you can think of that is "Airport or Airport Security" in the other column. Close this book and start listing for 10 minutes on your own. I'll wait here. After 10 minutes come back and compare your list to mine.

Disneyland	Airport or Airport Security
Characters	Lines
Mickey	Pat down
Minnie	X-ray machine
Donald	See through
Goofy	TSA, TSA pre-check
Happiest place on earth	Wand
Fast pass	Take shoes off
Smoked turkey leg	All metal, belt off
Food	Special pat down
Huge numbers of people	Expensive food
Teacups	Long lines
"Small World" ride—annoying song	Long waits
Long lines	Arrive early for check in
Long waits	Boarding pass
Someone taking pictures, Disneyland	Hug numbers of people
Charging for pictures	Someone taking pictures if you're into
Main Street, USA	some Eastern European countries
Tickets	terror attacks
Magic Kingdom	Tickets
Splash Moutain	Kids not having fun
Strollers	Wait for plane ride
Lots of kids	
Sunburn	
All day—several days	
Rides	

Step 3: Start Building Jokes

1. I noticed that standing in line at airport security was a lot like being in line at Disneyland: long lines, expensive food, some guy named Goofy wanting to pat you down.
2. I noticed that standing in line at airport security was a lot like being in line at Disneyland: long lines, expensive food, some goofy guy wanting to pat you down.
3. I noticed that standing in line at airport security was a lot like being in line at Disneyland. Disneyland has fast passes and airport security has the opposite.
4. I noticed that standing in line at airport security was a lot like being in line at Disneyland. The only way I can get through the pat down is to hum, "It's a small world."
5. I noticed that standing in line at airport security was a lot like being in line at Disneyland. It's the only way I can wait in line to enjoy way overpriced food and walk for hours to get where I'm going.
6. I noticed that standing in line at airport security was a lot like being in line at Disneyland. The only difference is I have more confidence in the security guard with the Mickey Mouse badge.
7. I noticed that standing in line at airport security was a lot like being in line at Disneyland. At Disneyland, having a fast pass is the bomb, and at the airport, saying "bomb" is a fast pass!
8. I noticed that standing in line at airport security was a lot like being in line at Disneyland. Everyone has the same look on their faces: "Can we go home yet?"
9. I noticed that standing in line at airport security was a lot like being in line at Disneyland. No one is really having fun ... even the ones paid to be there.

10. I noticed that standing in line at airport security was a lot like being in line at Disneyland. You pay a lot of money, wait in a long line, and end up entirely disappointed in the ride.

As a result of this free-association and combining the two ideas, I generated 10 possible jokes. I have no doubt there are even more jokes possible if I kept building on this list. The most important point here is to build your list of potential jokes as long as possible. You may need to search the Internet for more ideas related to your topic. Plus, you may encounter some current media items that will enhance the relevancy of the story you're telling. Try to write as many joke possibilities as you can. In the next chapter, we're going to talk about turning one laugh into two, three, four or more laughs using tags and toppers. The more joke possibilities you generate now, the more options you will have for tags and toppers later.

Generate Custom Laughs

Another way you can use the Simple Joke Writing System is to generate some custom laughs for your audience. Let's pretend you are doing a speech in Albuquerque. Hey, it could happen. You do some Internet searches and find this headline in the news: "Balloon Stolen at Albuquerque Balloon Fest." Let's follow the process and create a couple of custom humor ideas we could consider incorporating into our speech in Albuquerque.

Step 1: Isolate the Headline

"Balloon stolen at Albuquerque Balloon Fest"

Step 2: Generate an Association List of 2 or More Clearly Identifiable Subjects

Balloon	Thief/Crime/Stolen
Hot Air—hot air rises	Organized crime
Helium—funny voice	Gangs—Crips, Bloods (check their colors)
Huffing paint—like helium	Jail
Balloon animals—clowns—circus—circus tent	Reward
Air ship—Hindenburg	Wanted—"Wanted" poster
Blimp—Blimpie sandwiches	Arrest
Zeppelin—Led Zeppelin—hair metal band	Drive-by
Pilot	Victim
Weather balloon	Police—po po
Water balloon	Siren
Macy's day parade	Chase
Around the World in Eighty Days	Steal—stolen
Basket—gondola—wicker	Breaking and entering
Balloon rides	Get away—getaway car—drive the getaway
The noise they make	Criminal
Burner—flame	Famous criminals—Billy the Kid Museum
Propane—bbq—Hank Hill	(NM)
Heat	FBI
Fuel	CIA
Hitting power lines	ATF
Accidents	Drive-by shooting (float/fly by shooting)
Fiesta	Drunk driving (drunk flying)

Albuquerque Balloon Fiesta—largest	Highway patrol
First weekend in October	Border patrol (New Mexico? maybe)
Glow	Fleeing the law
Drift	Carjacking—LoJack—OnStar (OnStar for balloons)
Climb	Drug addicts—tweakers
	Addicts smuggle drugs in balloons up butts

Step 3: Start Building Jokes and Joke Possibilities.

Remember, go for 10! Or more!

11. A hot-air balloon was stolen at the annual Albuquerque Balloon Fiesta. The balloon is blue, has a US flag on the side, and was last seen floating east at less than 5 miles an hour.
12. In Albuquerque this week, a hot-air balloon was stolen. New Mexico police suspect a gang of hardened clowns.
13. In Albuquerque this week, a hot-air balloon was stolen. Seriously? Someone stole a balloon.... "OH, THE HUMANITY!"
14. In Albuquerque this week, a hot-air balloon was stolen. New Mexico police are in no hurry to locate the stolen balloon stating, "Give it time. What goes up, must come down."
15. In Albuquerque this week, a hot-air balloon was stolen. The victims gave chase but quickly gave up when the basket rose to 10 feet.
16. In Albuquerque this week, a hot-air balloon was stolen. The victims deny that the balloon was actually repossessed, stating they never missed a balloon payment.

17. In Albuquerque this week a hot-air balloon was stolen. The victims are blaming themselves for leaving the basket (gondola) unlocked.
18. In Albuquerque this week, a hot-air balloon was stolen. The victims were totally distraught, stating they only had one payment left ... only one remaining balloon payment.
19. In Albuquerque this week, a hot-air balloon was stolen. Which just goes to show.... Don't count your balloons before they're launched.
20. It happened during the city's annual balloon fiesta, which is expected to attract 700 balloons ... well, 699.
21. Albuquerque is known for a combination of weather patterns and geography that results in balloonists having great control over their balloons. That is, provided they aren't stolen.
22. The Albuquerque Balloon Fiesta is the most photographed event on the planet. So police find it very suspicious that "no one" saw anything.
23. In Albuquerque this week, a hot-air balloon was stolen. It happened during the city's annual balloon fiesta, and apparently everyone is really up in the air over it.
24. In Albuquerque this week, a hot-air balloon was stolen. Since being stolen, the balloon has been used for a variety of crimes, including a float-by shooting.
25. In Albuquerque this week, a hot-air balloon was stolen. The balloon has been recovered. It was found up on blocks and totally deflated.
26. During Albuquerque's Balloon Fiesta this week, a hot-air balloon was stolen. According to *US News* and *World Report*, the Albuquerque Balloon Fiesta is the

#2 thing to do in the city. The number one thing to do? Steal a balloon during the balloon fiesta.

Step 4: When You're Out of Ideas, Gather More Facts

In the case of the missing balloon, I went to the trusty Internet and did some research on Albuquerque and the balloon fiesta to get more facts. In addition, I read several stories related to the actual event to discover the balloon was blue and had a flag on the side. I got on a roll and generated 16 joke possibilities. As a result, I now have the option to pick the best joke, because quality comes from quantity.

The Process

While you're following The Laugh Generator Process, look for statements that have two clear, distinct ideas. Look for lines with similes and metaphors. Make a note to specifically come back and make your association lists for the two ideas contained in that line. From there, follow the process and write some potential jokes to generate more laughs. If you don't find any lines with two ideas, you can add a second idea by asking yourself, "What is this like?" Introduce that second idea into your speech, and then follow the process.

That's the basic process for writing jokes by combining two ideas, but the same technique can be used to write additional types of jokes. Two pieces of advice on using humor in speeches that I found constantly, yet unhelpful, was to exaggerate and use the Rule of Three. But as usual, none of the experts really explained exaggeration or the Rule of Three. I had to learn them from Jerry's classes and workshops.

Writing Exaggeration Jokes

Unfortunately, there's no magic bullet or secret formula to using exaggeration. The answer is to make lists, and, again, you're going to make two lists, just like before. In order to make an exaggeration joke, you need to know the thing you are talking about and the attribute you are going to exaggerate.

Person	Old
Birth certificate	Dinosaurs
Social Security number	Jurassic period
Parents	Bible
Going to schook, kindergarten	Dead Sea scrolls
High school	Revolutionary War
Learning to drive	Founding Fathers, 1776
Blood type	Model T
Eye color	Discontinued products
Height	
Weight	

Once you have two very complete lists, you can create jokes like this Phyllis Diller joke: "You know you're old when your birth certificate is on a scroll, and they've discontinued your blood type."

Again, you can see how combining one item from each list creates the joke. That's the heart of the Simple Joke Writing System. Now, how about that ever-present advice to use the Rule of Three? A lot of people talk about it, but how do you actually create a Rule of Three joke?

Writing a Rule of Three Joke

A Rule of Three Joke is created by, you guessed it, making lists. In the last chapter on The Laugh Generator Process, I shared an example from a coaching client talking about his boat. You remember Zeke's boat? On the rocks? You'll recall that one way I suggested he could have generated a laugh was to use this set-up line followed by the joke line: "I didn't want my boat to end up on the rocks, so I did what any captain would do ... I went to the liquor cabinet. Because, boat on the rocks bad, scotch on the rocks good."

The set-up line, "I did what any captain would do" is also the perfect set-up for a Rule of Three type joke. A Rule of Three joke has a setup line followed by two "examples" that set a pattern, support the setup line, and encourage a strong assumption. Finally, the "third" example breaks the pattern and generates the laugh.

What a Captain would do —Expected / Appropriate	Unexpected / Inappropriate
Set the anchor	Go to the liquor cabinet
Check the sail	Jump over board
Change course (head into the wind)	Start to cry uncontrollably
Take down the sail	
Trim the sail	
Adjust the halyard tension	

So, this joke is also a good candidate for using the Rule of Three structure to potentially heighten the tension and get a bigger laugh. The joke could look something like this: "I didn't want my boat to end up on the rocks, so I did what any captain would do ... I set a second anchor, pointed the stern into the wind, and went to the liquor cabinet. Because, boat on the rocks bad, scotch on the rocks good."

If I delivered the line this way, I would expect a laugh after "liquor cabinet" and the line after that would serve as a tag/topper to generate a second laugh. In addition to the tag/topper, there is also an opportunity here to do an act-out to generate more laughs.

7.

The Laugh Multiplier™: Turning One Laugh into Many

When you get a laugh, you can do two things. One, you can bask in people's giggles and be satisfied, or you can turn that single laugh into multiple laughs. The Laugh Multiplier Process involves the use of three tools to accomplish your task. Those three tools are

- Tags/Toppers
- Act-outs
- Callbacks

Tags/Toppers

In the world of stand-up comedy, the only measurement of success is laughs per minute. Let's start by discussing the value of tags and toppers, which are extremely common in that environment. Dick Vosburgh writes in the *Independent*, "According to *The Guinness Book of World Records*, each time Phyllis Diller exploded onto a nightclub floor, she notched up 12 laughs per minute, twice as many as her mentor Bob ("Rapid Robert") Hope."[62]

Are you curious how Phyllis Diller got those 12 laughs per minute? She explains how she did it in *The Comedy Bible* by Judy Carter: "I actually got twelve laughs in one minute from an audience. It was Bob Hope who noticed. Of course he would, he is such a constructionist. He goes for six a minute and he realized I was getting twelve. But there is a secret on how you do it! Topper, topper, topper."[63]

To understand and better use this laugh multiplier tool, let's take a closer look. In *Breaking Comedy's DNA*, my mentor, Jerry Corley, explains tags/toppers this way: "A tag or a topper is a comment on a punch line. It's one way a comedian can get more mileage out of a joke. So, instead of getting one laugh on the punch line, he can get three or four laughs."[64] Essentially, a tag or topper is a second punch line that comes when the audience thinks the joke is already finished. Which is why Mel Helitzer, author of *Comedy Writing Secrets*, says that toppers are great for keeping up the energy.[65]

Now that we have heard from the experts, let's take a look at some examples of tags/toppers in action. In my speech about riding my bicycle 100 miles by mistake, I share this line: "We were about to embark on a bicycle ride with over 8,000 other bicyclists. 8,000 Cyclists! That is a lot of spandex! And that was just what *I* was wearing." I always get a laugh after "spandex." I follow that up (tag it) by saying "and that's just what *I* was wearing," which generates a second laugh. The tag provides a new surprise where I am referring to myself as being a big guy.

Here's an example from one of my favorites, Brian Kiley.

"I'm happily married and know that I'm lucky because 50% of married people say that they're unhappily married. This is according to a poll I took earlier tonight at my house." (Audience laughter) "What's her problem?"

He follows the laugh by using the tag, "What's her problem?" and generates a second laugh. Then he says, "When I first met my wife, I didn't think I had a shot with her at all because she was just so pregnant." (Audience laughter) "That's not normally my type." Again, the laughter is followed by a tag "That's not normally my type," which is a comment on her being pregnant. Essentially, the tag provides a new surprise twist.

Kiley continues, "And I thought I had a morbid streak until I met my wife. Like I think about my own death sometimes. She thinks about my death constantly." (Audience laughter) "That's all she talks about." (Audience laughter) The tag this time serves to add to the surprise, rather than provide a new surprise. That's not really important, just a nice subtlety. Either way, Brian is an expert at turning one laugh into two.

Does the tag/topper technique have a place in public speaking? Without a doubt and to show you how it can be used, let's look at one of the most popular TED Talks of all time by Sir Ken Robinson:

> I have an interest in education. Actually, what I find is everybody has an interest in education. Don't you? I find this very interesting. If you're at a dinner party, and you say you work in education—Actually, you're not often at dinner parties, frankly.
>
> (Laughter)[66]
>
> If you work in education, you're not asked.
>
> (Laughter)

How Are Tags/Toppers Created?

In The Laugh Generator and The Simple Joke Writing System chapters, I encouraged you to try to get to 10 possibilities. Remember "Go for 10"? This is one of the reasons to do it. By creating that many options, you now have several possibilities in reserve, so look there first. If you don't find anything obvious, the next step is to go through The Laugh Generator Process again with the complete joke. When I was refining the 100-mile bike ride speech to win the contest, I had this line:

> We were about to embark on a bicycle ride with over 8,000 other bicyclists. 8,000 cyclists!

I used The Laugh Generator process and came up with this line:

That is a lot of spandex!

From there, I realized the assumption was that the spandex referred to the 8,000 cyclists. I recognized the assumption was "who" was wearing the spandex. So, I twisted the assumption to mean me, instead of the cyclists, resulting in the line, "And that was just what *I* was wearing." The second place you can find tags/toppers is while you are on stage, in the moment. One of the reasons you want to at least record the audio of every performance is to capture the improvisational moments that will happen on stage.

For example, while giving a speech about Amarillo, Texas I had an improv moment that created a tag/topper that also became a keeper. You'll be hearing more about Amarillo (how exciting, right?) since I use the entire speech as an example later. Specifically, I was talking about how Texans speak: "The other thing you're going to hear a lot of is, 'all git-out.' (laugh) It means, 'to great degree, exceedingly or as much as possible.' Rick's speech was funnier than all git-out. (laugh) If you don't believe that, well then, get out!" (laugh) I wasn't planning on saying, "If you don't believe that, well then, get out!" That line came to me when I heard myself say "git-out," and I realized in that moment how close it was to "get out." I combined that and created the tag/topper in the moment.

One quick note before we move on to act-outs is the need to pause. Make sure you allow time for each laugh to complete before revealing the next tag/topper. Wait it out, and you'll get the best laughs.

Act-Outs

Jerry Corley explained act-outs in his book, *Breaking Comedy's DNA*:

> An extension of the tag or topper is the "act-out." In stand-up comedy, act-out is King. An act-out is a name used to label physicalizing and/or verbalizing a situation that you set up or alluded to in your comedy.
>
> By acting out a joke you not only introduce a new element, you also introduce a new dimension and take a two-dimensional act and turn it into a three-dimensional act by making it come alive.[67]

Act-outs aren't solely for stand-up comedy though. And that's a great thing. Jerry was right (he usually is)—the act-out is KING. All hail the King. Judy Carter, in her book *The Message of You*, shares this idea: "Using the act-out technique is a must. It's a technique that should be used constantly throughout your entire speech...."[68] Sir Ken Robinson incorporates act-out in his popular Ted Talk. His act-out isn't filled with body language but simple dialogue. Here is an excerpt from the transcript.

> 6:33 Actually, we lived in a place called Snitterfield, just outside Stratford, which is where Shakespeare's father was born. Are you struck by a new thought? I was. You don't think of Shakespeare having a father, do you? Do you? Because you don't think of Shakespeare being a child, do you? Shakespeare being seven? I never thought of it. I mean, he was seven at some point. He was in somebody's English class, wasn't he?
>
> 6:54 (Laughter)
>
> 7:01 How annoying would that be?
>
> 7:03 (Laughter)
>
> 7:10 "Must try harder."

7:11 (Laughter)
7:15 Being sent to bed by his dad, you know, to Shakespeare, "Go to bed, now! And put the pencil down."
7:21 (Laughter)
7:22 "And stop speaking like that."
7:24 (Laughter)
7:28 "It's confusing everybody."
7:29 (Laughter)[69]

Above, Jerry Corley mentioned that act-out is an extension of the tag/topper. Notice at 7:01 the line, "How annoying would that be?" Technically that line is a tag/topper, but it sets up the opportunity for an act-out. Essentially, by asking the question, we have an opportunity for Sir Ken to show us via act-out how annoying it really is. Using that combination of a tag/topper and act-out, he took the one laugh and turned it into six laughs. Notice that he didn't need a lot of words to do it, and if you watch the video, you will plainly see his act-out was simply the dialogue of the scenario.

Also, one thing strikes me when I watch the video: Sir Ken did the unthinkable. What is the unthinkable? The unthinkable, in the eyes of many fluff experts, is laughing at your own jokes. He does it, and his audience doesn't mind. In fact, watch the video. You'll see some of the laughs he receives are because people enjoy him enjoying his own joke.

In my speech about Amarillo, Texas I make use of an act-out this way:

There is an upside though. Amarillo is nationally ranked for some of the cleanest air in the country. Thanks to the wind. (laugh)

You got trash? Throw it up. (laugh)

Enjoy the trash, Oklahoma. (laugh)

Put that on the Chamber website. (laugh)

In this example, each line is a tag/topper, but I enhanced them by adding an act-out. When I said "Throw it up," I gestured appropriately. When I said, "Enjoy the trash, Oklahoma," I cupped my hand to my mouth as if I was calling to Oklahoma.

You can use act-outs anywhere in your speech or presentation. They don't have to be used only with humor, but, in our case, we're focusing on generating laughs. One way to identify the opportunity to do an act-out is when you say something, the audience laughs, and you follow up by showing them what you just told them by acting it out.

In the "Simple Joke Writing" chapter, I shared this statement from a speech given by a coaching client: "I noticed that standing in line at Airport security was a lot like being in line at Disneyland." Well, that line is back for another example because it's a nice setup for an act-out. Because this is straight from her personal experience; all she has to do is "show us" what she saw that triggered the thought in her head. Plus, when you combine an act-out with one of the jokes, you can generate a really nice laugh. For example: "I noticed that standing in line at Airport security was a lot like being in line at Disneyland: the only way I can get through the pat down is to hum, 'It's a Small World.'"

An act-out for that joke could be as simple as standing with arms outstretched and humming the tune. That is all it would take to turn one laugh into two. Plus, that act-out is also a nice setup to be used again later in the form of a callback.

Callback

The third tool in The Laugh Multiplier is the callback. Just like tags/toppers and act-outs, callbacks are commonplace in stand-up comedy. Callbacks are also often in speeches, too, but in this case, we are specifically using them to turn one laugh into several. In *Breaking Comedy's DNA*, Jerry Corley defines a callback in this way: "A word, expression, or joke that is a reference back to one performed earlier in a comedian's act. It could be referred to by the same comedian or another comedian who's performing in the same show."[70]

Callbacks are popular with an audience because they help the comic develop a special intimacy with the audience.

> *A callback is when you make a reference, later in your act, to something you said earlier.*
> **Judy Carter**

There is a beautiful example of the callback available on the Internet. Search for "2014 World Champion of Public Speaking Dananjaya Hettiarachchi," and you'll be able to watch his speech, "I see something." As you watch, notice at 3 minutes and 50 seconds he says, "I see something in you, but I don't know what it is," and he gets a laugh. He says it again at 5 minutes and 50 seconds. The laugh is even bigger. And then again at 6 minutes and 40 seconds, he says it again with a bit of a twist. The laugh is even bigger. In fact, he had to stop half way through the line and wait for the laughs to subside before continuing. And finally, at 7 minutes 35 seconds, he concludes with that line again, and lots of laughter.

To effectively use a callback to generate another laugh, all you have to do is make a note when the audience laughs. This is easy to do because you have the transcript available. Next, simply repeat the line again later. You may have to modify it slightly to fit the context, but when you do it well, you'll generate another laugh.

8.

The 7 Deadly Humor Mistakes Speakers Make and How to Avoid Them

The purpose of this book is to help speakers have fun and to mesmerize, fascinate, and engage. To achieve that purpose, I need to point out some of the mistakes I see speakers making. And because I know I need to be a coach and not just a critic, I've included how you can avoid these mistakes.

Mistake #1—Not Using Humor or Trying to Ignore Its Important Benefits

By far, the biggest mistake is not using humor at all or not using it enough. For some reason, people are happy to dismiss the idea with a flippant, "I'm just not funny" or "I'm just not naturally funny." Hear me clearly: NO ONE is naturally funny. Research has shown over and over again that, if we want to improve at something, we must practice and practice, which is, in fact, more important than any "natural" talent.

Since I'm speaking to "speakers," allow me to put it this way. When I was in sales and needed to recruit salespeople, I got the same answer: "I'm just not a salesperson." As a member of Toastmasters, I invite people to meetings all the time, but I get the same reason from them for not accepting my invitation: "I'm just not a speaker." Even if you don't call yourself a speaker, if you're a teacher, a salesperson, a preacher, or a pastor, the benefits of using humor make it a necessity. Go back and review "The 7 Reasons Humor Is a Must or YOU FAIL" and commit to practicing the skill of humor.

Mistake #2—Using Street Jokes, Book Jokes, or Canned Jokes

Street jokes, book jokes, or canned jokes are what most humor experts are referring to when they advise people, "Don't start with a joke." The reason I think using these types of jokes is a mistake is that they usually start with "Did you hear the one about...?" or some similar cliché. When your audience hears a typical set-up or opening, they automatically know a joke is coming; they've been conditioned. Unfortunately, you've just established that the rest of your presentation may be as unoriginal as the old joke you just told.

If you want, you can try to modernize the cliché set-up, drop the set-up altogether, or try using The Laugh Generator Process to find the natural laugh points in your speech, presentation, and stories. You'll reap all of the benefits of using humor without using canned jokes that will work against you.

Mistake #3—"Borrowing" Someone Else's Jokes

James Altucher wrote an excellent article entitled, "How to Be the Best Public Speaker on the Planet." In it, he advises people to study comedians. Great advice. Until he says this:

> When possible, I will directly steal a joke from whatever comedian I'm watching. If they've tested out the joke, then it's probably a good one and will work for me as well.
>
> I even practice imitating their timing. The way

they pause, the way they change voices and move around the stage, everything.

Comedians are the best public speakers and are up against the most brutal audiences so you MUST study comedians.[71]

Stealing jokes is just as bad as using canned or book jokes. Do you really want to risk even one person in the audience recognizing that you "borrowed" a joke? Credibility? Instantly gone. You can use jokes but give attribution to the comedian who wrote it. You attribute quotes? Books? Other ideas? Right? Giving credit not only shows you are well read, but it enhances your credibility, reputation, and positioning as an expert.

Rather than "borrowing" jokes, why not use The Laugh Generator Process to come up with your own jokes quickly and efficiently?

Mistake #4—Being Impatient and Giving Up Too Soon

Thomas A. Edison, inventor of the light bulb, said, "Our greatest weakness lies in giving up. The most certain way to succeed is always to try just one more time." Edison is famous for not only his inventions, but also his attitude: "I have not failed 10,000 times. I have not failed once. I have succeeded in proving that those 10,000 ways will not work."[72] I appreciate Tom's (yea, I call him Tom.) attitude, because I myself have succeeded in finding 10,000 diets that will not work.

When I talk about giving up too soon, I'm talking about giving up too soon on both the joke and on getting better. As you try The Laugh Generator Process, I encourage you to try to find 10 possible laugh lines.

I developed the habit of "digging deeper" from my comedy

mentor, Jerry Corley. He developed the same habit from another comic's encouragement. Jerry told me he was touring with a guy who used to be the head writer on a comedy show.

"I wrote a joke about Congress that I was pretty proud of."

Then Jerry said, "I told this writer my joke. He said, 'dig deeper.' I wrote another one, he said, 'dig deeper.'"

Apparently, the writer kept repeating his "dig deeper" advice to Jerry until he had put three hours in on the joke.

"By the time I was done," said Jerry. "I had 30 lines for that one joke, and the more I worked, the funnier they got. Because of that one event, I started digging deep all the time. It wasn't long before I got 30 lines in two hours, then in just an hour."[73]

Jerry isn't the only one who encourages us not to give up too soon. I promised you earlier that I would share Gene Perret's advice on a concept he calls "overwriting."

> I advocate overwriting. Why? Because it forces you to continue to write and get some of the obvious jokes out of the way. The more you write, the more creative your concepts seem to become. Also, in overwriting, you give yourself the luxury of selecting only your best jokes. For instance, if you need three solid jokes to introduce someone at a banquet, write ten or twelve and then SELECT the best three. If you write only three, that's all you'll have to choose from.[74]

Once you have the joke you're going to try out, you might be tempted to trash the joke the first time it fails to get the kind of laughs you expect. Don't throw it out yet. It's not a three day old doughnut that's dry and hard. Try The Laugh Troubleshooter Process to help you tweak your wording, structure, and punch line. I recommend taking a joke through The Laugh Troubleshooter Process three times before you throw it out.

Finally, we come to the third area where people give up too soon. Daniel Coyle shares this tip in his *Little Book of Talent*. In Tip #48, Give a New Skill a Minimum of Eight Weeks, he says no one can be "proficient in any skill in eight weeks." His advice: "Don't make judgments too early. Keep at it, even if you don't feel immediate improvement."[75] In the case of adding humor to your speeches and presentations, I contend that we aren't just talking about one skill but several. So, maybe consider giving yourself more than eight weeks. To reinforce my point, take a look at "Becoming the Funniest You" and "The 90-Day Humor Improvement Plan" in the resources at the end of this book.

Mistake #5—Not Testing Out Material Ahead of Time

My comedy mentor said George Carlin told him, "I know with 98 percent accuracy that a joke is funny BEFORE I take the stage." That is impressive. I have no doubt that as you practice and improve your skills, you too will know with greater certainty which jokes will work. Until then, here's the solution.

Test it first.

In stand-up comedy, we can test jokes out using an open mic, made for trying out new bits of material and playing with our delivery and timing. In his book, *Little Bets: How Breakthrough Ideas Emerge from Small Discoveries*, Peter Sims shares this enlightened analysis of Chris Rock's success: "In front of audiences of say 50 people, he will show up unannounced, carrying a yellow legal note pad with joke ideas scribbled on it. It's like boxing training camp."[76] Comics like Rock use open mics to test out drafts of their material. As a public speaker, you can use Toastmasters meetings the exact same way. The

Toastmasters program includes the *Competent Communicator Manual*, which contains 10 different projects. Each project is allocated a five- to seven-minute time frame—the perfect amount of time to try out your latest humorous story.

Mistake #6—Writing for the Page and Not the Stage

This mistake is a common one for speakers and actually goes beyond using humor. Somehow, a speech has to "get written." For some people, that means actually sitting down to write. The way we talk is very different from the way we write though. That can be a problem for live humor. Words intended for the ear should be different from words intended for the eye. Speeches depend more on delivery and the nonverbal elements of speech than written essays or books do. As a result, very often, when you read a joke that's meant to be delivered on a stage, you might think, "This joke isn't funny." Plus, the delivery mechanism of written words allows readers to reread a passage if they didn't understand the meaning immediately. No such safety net exists with delivering a joke live.

The first step in The Laugh Generator Process is to actually deliver your speech, presentation, or story. In that way, you can learn to avoid the mistake of creating a joke that works in writing but not in person. Another way you can learn how to write for the stage and not for the page is to write your speech as though you are speaking. As I'm writing, I will say sentences out loud for myself to verify the structure is close to matching the way I would say it. I do this frequently (luckily, my cats think I'm talking to them), knowing that I need to get the main ideas down, but also knowing that the first draft is really when I deliver my speech and my jokes for the first time.

Mistake #7—Starting Out by Asking, "What Is Funny?"

Comedian Greg Wilson says, "The more you try to chase comedy the further away from you it gets." Almost like chasing that cute girl in seventh grade homeroom. His statement is why one of my favorite vaguleralities offered by so-called humor experts is to start by asking yourself, "What's funny?" Why is asking such a question vague, bad advice? Because although it sounds like a good idea, asking yourself what's funny is the surest method for getting yourself stuck in writer's block.

> *Humor is tragedy plus time.*
> **Mark Twain**

Plus, starting out looking for the funny is a great way to end up being absurd. Jerry Corley says, "Comedy is heightened reality. It's not complete absurdity. It's taking what's real and putting it under a microscope or a magnifying glass for the audience to see clearly."[77]

My improv instructor often told us that comedy is trying to get from point A to point B and encountering obstacles. The idea is simple. Comedy has to have a foundation in truth and reality. Comedian Jerry Corley says, "Make sure you start with something real before you try to turn it into something funny."[78] The Laugh Generator Process and the joke-writing process will show you how to take the truth and make it funny. That's what Mark Twain means when he says, "Get your facts first, then you can distort them as you please."

> *Comedy is truth and pain.*
> **John Vorhaus**

One final note, as soon as you start trying to think, "What's funny?" you begin engaging your internal editor. Once you start listening to that critical voice, your creativity shuts down—the exact opposite of what you want to happen.

> *If I got a paper cut, that's a tragedy. If you fell down an open manhole and died, that's comedy.*
> **Mel Brooks**

So those are the seven mistakes I see speakers making. Are they really deadly? Not in the real sense of the word, but your ability to create and present humorous material will be on life support, nearly flat lining, gasping for each breath. Okay, maybe I'm being a wee bit dramatic. Fortunately, you now know how to identify and avoid these mistakes by using the processes and tools in this book. As a result, you'll soon become a funnier you.

9.

Delivery and The Laugh Amplifier™

Generating laughs and being funny is a combination of what you say and how you say it. In this section, we're going to look at the essentials of delivery—how you say it. Delivery can add to or detract from your humor. It consists of two major components: your voice and your body.

As you look out at your audience and see their faces loaded with anticipation, the very first thing you need to do is smile. Timothy Koegel shares why in *The Exceptional Presenter*: "A smile eases tension and creates a warm environment. A smile lights up one's eyes. A smile says, 'I've done this before, I'm confident and I'll do my best to make this an interesting and informative session.'"[79] Once you smile, you're ready to deliver. And as I said, delivery is more than what you say. Darlene Price, President of *Well Said*, Inc. and author of Well Said! , explains, "Separate from the actual words used, these nonverbal elements of your voice include voice tone, pacing, pausing, volume, inflection, pitch, and articulation."[80]

Susan Weinschenk, author of *100 Things Every Presenter Needs to Know about People*, states: "People react not only to your message, but to your voice, stance, facial expressions, and hand movements. A special field called paralinguistics studies how information is communicated in addition to the words you say."[81] And how you say them is even more important when it comes to being funny. In her ebook, *What I Learned by Watching 15 Speakers in 2015*, Laurie Guest, a Certified Speaking Professional (CSP), talks about Ron Culberson who is also a CSP and a member of the National Speaker's Association Speaker Council of Peers Award for Excellence Hall of Fame (CPAE):

Well, he had them laughing in the first two minutes with a joke that was so dumb, I actually rolled my eyes. But at the same time, I couldn't help but laugh because of his delivery, facial expressions, and the pure joy he showed when he landed just the right punch line.

I watched him demonstrate what he has been teaching me over the last few years. It isn't so much what you say, but how you say it. We all know this, but it deserves a reminder because it is so important. Our words are just words until we attach emotion, meaning, and application.

That's what causes a reaction in the listener. In the case of Ron's audience, he delivered the words in a hot pocket of humor.[82]

Let's take a look at some of the nonverbal components of your voice as it relates to delivery jokes and humor.

Tone

According to Mark Waldman and Andrew Newberg, M.D. in *Psychology Today*, "Researchers at the University of Amsterdam found that expressions of anger, contempt, disgust, fear, sadness, and surprise were better communicated through vocal tone than facial expression."[83]

Those researchers must not have had mothers because if they had, they wouldn't have had to do the research. My mother's mantra was, "It's not what you say but the *WAY* you say it." I've never forgotten the lesson she taught me and my brother, that tone carries more meaning than the words we use. How could I forget it? I only heard it 147,273 times. I'm NOT exaggerating. My mother told me a million times not to exaggerate.

> 60% of all human communication is nonverbal body language; 30% is your tone, so that means 90% of what you're saying ain't coming out of your mouth.
> **Alex "Hitch" Hitchens**

Pacing and Speed

The number one point to keep in mind about comedy and humor is that a confused audience does not laugh. Therefore, when it comes to your pacing and speed, you may have to adjust your speed and pacing based on your material. If your content is technical and complicated, you should probably slow down. Also, speaking more slowly will help your audience understand if you have an accent, dialect, or other similar quality. I say "similar" because I recently heard a speaker who was extremely difficult to understand. I had to really concentrate to hear and discern what she was saying. And, it wasn't because I'd had too many beers. On the way home, my wife mentioned that the speaker had dentures that didn't fit properly. My wife is a therapist who works primarily in an assisted living setting, so she was able to recognize the reason I had a difficult time understanding some words. That speaker is someone who needs to be conscious of her speed and pace in order to ensure that the audience can understand her.

Pause Timing—The Art of the Pause

In addition to being funny, timing is something that most "experts" tout as one of the "unteachables." According to film actress, Deepika Padukone, "Comic timing is something which you either have it in you, or you don't. You have to have a good sense of humour to be able to understand it. A split second can make you lose the punch." I disagree. Timing can be taught and learned, too. In "Humor Demystified" (chapter three), I explain how generating a laugh is as simple as recognizing the assumptions and expectations in the mind of your listener and then creating a twist to create something new. Hold on, here comes a baseball quote. Yogi Berra said, "You don't have to swing hard to hit a homerun. If you got the timing, it'll go."

Timing, then, is pausing long enough to ensure the assumption or expectation is affirmed in the mind of your audience, but not so long that they have time to figure out the joke. Consider this joke I wrote: "A nutritionist told me to lose weight. I should eat half, she said, and throw the other half away. I can't do that; it's wrong. There are people starving in this world, and if I don't eat that other half ... I could be one of them." The ellipsis (three dots) is used to indicate a longer than normal pause. During that pause, the audience is beginning to fill in the blank; doing so is human nature and can't be avoided. This is the listening gap I talked about earlier. Give the audience time to fill in the blank and then you drop the twist (punch line), which generates the laugh.

Volume

Similar to speed is the volume of your voice. The volume required is heavily influenced by the size of the room and ambient noise. If you're using a microphone, pay attention if the mic is "hot," meaning it's too loud. I attended a training recently and the speaker was using a microphone, although the room probably didn't require it. He didn't adjust his volume to the level of the microphone and was consistently too loud. Yes, too loud can be an issue too.

Enunciation and Articulation—Speak Clearly

Humor and mumbling go together like oil and water. You won't generate laughs if you mumble because your audience needs to clearly understand what you are saying so that they create an assumption in their mind. In my case, I say the word "picture," and it sounds a lot like I'm saying "pitcher." I slur the word a little and as a result, when I'm telling the story about my wife and taking a picture while we were hiking, I have to be extra careful to enunciate and articulate the "c" in the word "picture" to avoid confusion.

Facial Expression

When I was in sales, my manager would often ask me if I was having a good time. I'd reply, "Yes" and he'd reply, "You should tell your face." My reply was, "You tell my face, I'm thinking." Basically he was telling me that my facial expression was revealing a different story. According to a study by researchers at Ohio State University, the human face is capable of communicating 21 distinct emotions.[84] The key point is that your face reveals what you are really feeling, so be aware of your expressions and use them to your advantage. The goal is to aim for congruity between your face and the material. Incongruity could cause your audience confusion and result in less laughter.

Neuroscience is constantly revealing new findings related to how we communicate and how we can enhance our communication. In her book, *100 Things Every Presenter Needs to Know about People*, Susan M. Weinschenk shares some information about a specific area of the brain called the fusiform area (FFA). Basically, the FFA allows us to quickly identify faces and interpret emotions. The FFA allows us to derive meaning from faces: "Showing emotion—whether happy, sad, disgusted, or afraid—will communicate more quickly and deeply than words can."[85]

Body Language and Gestures

People instantly and unconsciously "read" and assign meaning to your body positions, movement, and gestures. Susan M. Weinschenk explains it this way:

> Everyone "talks" with their hands to some extent. Some people's hand-talking or gesturing matches their message well. Other people have a tendency to make overly large gestures that can be distracting. Others don't use their hands much at all. No matter which camp you fall into, it's important to pay attention to your hand gestures while you are presenting, and perhaps try out some new ones.[86]

Vanessa Van Edwards on her "Science of People" blog and in *Huffington Post* says,

> In our human behavior research lab, we analyzed thousands of hours of TED talks and found one striking pattern: The most viral TED Talkers spoke with their words AND their hands. Specifically, we analyzed the top and bottom Ted Talks:
>
> The least popular TED Talkers used an average

of 272 hand gestures during the 18 minute talk. The most popular TED Talkers used an average of 465 hand gestures—that's almost double!

Wow, 465 hand gestures in an 18-minute talk. I'm thinking "JAZZ HANDS!"

What Do You Do When the Audience Is Laughing?

While the audience is laughing you want to amplify the laughter using the Laugh Amplifier Process. As you finish saying the punch line (the final words you say right before you expect the audience to laugh), you have to be willing to pause and wait for that laugh. Often, if the audience doesn't start laughing immediately, we fear the joke didn't work, so we start talking. Don't do it. Give the joke time to breathe and the laughter time to start. You need to pause. The very first step in amplifying a laugh is to pause and wait for the laughs and keep pausing as long as there are laughs. If the audience is laughing, you shouldn't be talking or trying to talk. As soon as you start your next word, the audience will stop laughing in order to hear what you have to say. Trying to talk when the audience is laughing is called "stepping on the laugh." It's a common problem in the beginning. If you "step on the laugh," you can actually train your audience to not laugh. Yes, I've done it.

Craig Valentine, author of *World Class Speaking* states:
When they laugh, do you stop and let them finish? If not, guess what happens psychologically to your audience? They say to themselves, "Well shoot—if he keeps cutting me off, I won't laugh next time." Let

them laugh, and let them laugh fully. When they get to the end of their laugh, move on to your next thought....

Give them that experience. Wait it out, and then move on.[88]

Stepping on the laugh doesn't just happen verbally; we communicate with our face and body, so it's possible to step on the laugh non-verbally. When the audience is laughing, stay in the character or state of mind you were in when you delivered the line. That means your facial expression and body language should match the emotion of the joke. And if you use your face to exaggerate the emotion of the joke, you can amplify the laugh even more. So while the audience is laughing, you can play with facial expressions.

Facial expressions are the second step in The Laugh Amplifier Process. In the first step of the process, you need to stay congruent and match your body language with the tone of the joke. From there, you can play with a variety of exaggerated body reactions. My favorite source for more detail on the following reactions comes from the book, *The Joke's on You: How to Write Comedy by Stephen Hoover*:
- Deadpan
- Slow blink
- Double take
- Eye bulge
- Smirk[89]

Is It Okay to Laugh at Your Own Joke? Absolutely!

A common warning with regard to using humor in speeches is that one is to never laugh at one's own jokes. To this I say, "Forget it. Don't worry about it and have a good time!" My comedy coach and mentor constantly reminds his students that the "audience is in the same frame of mind as the performer." That reminder is a very practical way of describing the purpose of mirror neurons that I talked about earlier. Practical explanations are always great. In *How to Get People to Do Stuff*, Susan M. Weinschenk describes how people imitate each other's feelings:

> Not only do your facial expressions and body language communicate information and affect how people react to you and your message, they may also cause people to feel a certain way.
>
> People imitate what they see. If you're smiling, those around you will tend to smile. If you're energetic, they'll be energetic too.
>
> Whatever your thoughts and feelings are, they're communicated through your words, tone of voice, and body language, and picked up and felt by the person you're talking to.[90]

I've already mentioned that Sir Ken Robinson's TED Talk is one of the most popular TED Talks of all time. Well, in that talk, Sir Ken laughs at his own jokes. He is having a good time sharing the stories and laughs with his audience, and his audience, no doubt, laughs more because he is laughing with them. It's okay to laugh at your own jokes because laughter is social activity and our brains are wired to detect laughter in others and to laugh with them. You've heard it before, thanks to mirror neurons, "Laughter is contagious."

Make sure you're having a good time and put a smile on your face. Then the key is to make sure each element of your delivery matches the intent of your joke and story. Just one piece not matching can cause confusion and a confused audience doesn't laugh.

10.

The Laugh Troubleshooter™ Process

Thomas J. Watson, Chairman of IBM in 1943, says, "If you want to increase your success rate, double your failure rate." He knows what he's talking about. Watson also said, "I think there is a world market for maybe five computers." Seriously? Five computers? Of course, at the time each computer was the size of a house so I'll cut him some slack.

What do you do when you don't get the laugh you expected? First thing, don't panic, look frustrated, get angry, or accuse the audience of missing it. When I talked about delivery earlier, I said the audience is in the same emotional state as you, the performer. I heard this message from my comedy mentor, Jerry, over and over again. So how does that apply to the audience not laughing? Timothy Koegel nails the answer: "If you say something that is intended to be funny, enjoy the moment. Keep your head and eyes up. If they laugh or smile, that's wonderful. If they don't, simply move on to your next point."[91]

So smile and move on, but then take ownership of the failed joke and just accept that they didn't laugh.

To begin our discussion on troubleshooting a joke, let's go back and look at how you learned to generate laughs. To generate a laugh, you create or recognize the assumption/expectation in the audience's mind and then twist it to mean something new. How can this go wrong? The major reason an audience doesn't laugh is they are confused. And remember, a confused audience doesn't laugh. Whenever I'm helping a comedian or speaker with a joke that hasn't been getting laughs, the issue is usually with clarity. Most of the time, just like my client's audience, I can't understand what the speaker is trying to say. In other words, I don't understand the setup to the joke or even the punch line.

The two possible points of confusion:
1. The assumption/expectation isn't clear.
2. The twist isn't clear.

The best time to troubleshoot a joke is after the presentation and preferably by reviewing the video. If there isn't a video available, how about the audio? Frankly, if you don't have at least the audio, there's no point in trying to troubleshoot a joke; you just can't troubleshoot from memory. As I shared earlier, memory is the third thing to go.

When you do have audio or audio and video, have the audio transcribed so you can see the exact words you used. To troubleshoot, you are going to analyze the exact words and ask yourself seven key questions:

1. Are All the Right Words in the Right Places?

The first step is to check and make sure all the words necessary for the joke were included. Did the audience have the information needed to make an assumption? It's possible to leave out words that are necessary for my audience to clearly understand the joke. I've done it and still do it. Here is an example from Brian Kiley that's funny: "So we have two kids. We're very fortunate, a few years ago, my wife and I, we were told that we were unable to have children ... by our landlord." But it's not funny this way: "So we have two kids. We're very fortunate, a few years ago, my wife and I, we were told that we couldn't rent a house if we had kids by our landlord." It's also not funny this way: "So we have two kids. We're very fortunate, a few years ago, our landlord told my wife and I, we were unable to have children."

In the joke, Brian Kiley uses the phrase "unable to have kids," which really reinforces the assumption that the reason is biological. In the first unfunny example, not only is the joke spoiled by the word usage, it's also spoiled by the word order. The same is true for the second example.

2. Did You Give All the Necessary Facts?

Brian Kiley: We always called my grandfather poppy because of his opium.

For this joke to work, the audience has to know that poppy isn't just a slang term for father, but that it's also a type of flower used to create opium. And the audience would need to know that opium is a highly addictive narcotic. This joke would be one of those that gets a laugh sometimes but not others, usually because of the age of your audience. If the joke you're troubleshooting falls into that category, make a note of the audience demographics that laugh and the audiences that don't laugh. You'll be able to spot trends and adjust the jokes by giving additional information ahead of the joke to ensure the audience has all the facts necessary. For Brian's joke above, one possible addition to help the audience "get it" would be to hint that his grandfather has a bit of an addictive personality. Like this, "My grandfather has an addictive personality. We call him poppy because of his opium.

Take a look at this Rodney Dangerfield joke: "My wife's a water sign. I'm an earth sign. Together we make mud." For this joke to work, the audience needs to know that Dangerfield is referring to astrological signs and that astrological signs are categorized as earth, water, fire, and air. The joke only works with these words. If we tried to say, "My wife is a Cancer and I'm a Virgo. Together we make mud," the joke wouldn't work. It doesn't work this way either: "My wife's a water sign and I'm a Virgo. Together we make mud." For the audience to laugh, they need to be with you on the journey of the joke. Don't get ahead of them and don't let them get ahead of you.

One day my wife and I were at the grocery store. While we were at the cash register, we noticed a gentleman eating lunch and working on his computer with his grocery cart nearby. He had some soap in his grocery cart.

Here are the facts:
He was working on his laptop computer
He had a grocery cart with soap
My wife said, "Looks like he's laundering his money."
Soap › Computer › Assumed he was doing banking › "Money Laundering"
I said, "Probably just cleaning his hard drive."
Soap › Computer › "Cleaning Hard Drive"

In this example, my wife made an assumption that the man was working financial or banking related tasks. The facts didn't support her assumption as well because we really didn't know what he was doing. If I told this joke from the stage, the version with the assumptive leap about doing banking, it would likely get fewer laughs than the version with the assumptive leap about cleaning his computer's hard drive.

3. Did You Leave a Little Puzzle the Audience Needs to Solve?

Brian Kiley explains: "I've got a lot of problems. I have that problem that sometimes in the middle of the night that I'll stop breathing. It's not sleep apnea. It's the other where your wife's holding a pillow over your face." In this joke, Brian is essentially saying his wife tries to kill him in his sleep. He's saying it without saying it; it's the joke's subtext. If Brian delivered the joke this way, there's nothing to get: "I've got a lot of problems. I have that problem that sometimes in the middle of the night that I'll stop breathing. It's not sleep apnea. My wife's trying to kill me." In this second version, the joke is too direct and "on the nose" to be funny. By leaving the little puzzle and letting the audience figure out his wife's intention, Kiley allows for the laugh to happen.

Here is an example from George, one of my coaching clients: "There's an old woman behind bulletproof glass and on the glass are two signs: one sign with room prices—one hour, two hours, three hours, and ... all night. And then next to that, a second sign that says, 'Absolutely NO prostitution'—with an exclamation point!" There's a little room for a laugh at the incongruity of the two signs. However, there's an opportunity to give away less information and let the audience work a little to get the joke. Specifically, the room prices started at "one hour" and ended at "all night." That word order clearly spells out the situation. I suggested he rearrange the wording to allow for the puzzle to be solved by the audience. Here is my suggestion:

There's an old woman behind bulletproof glass and on the glass are two signs. The first has room prices listed ... one rate for all night and one rate by the hour.

The second sign (make fingers into a square to look like a sign) "Absolutely NO prostitution" ... without prior approval.

In the edited version, the room prices start with one rate for all night, which is what would be expected, and then the joke ends with the twist of "by the hour" to trigger the surprise and the first laugh. Next, the second sign contradicts the prices sign and this incongruity triggers the second laugh. The final twist of "without prior approval" is considered a tag/topper and provides the third laugh. For more on tags/toppers, read The Laugh Multiplier (chapter seven).

Does being this picky about word choice and arrangement matter that much? Well, these certainly make a difference in this case. The first configuration had one laugh with 42 words. The second configuration had three laughs with 50 words.

Here's an example from Zeke, whom I introduced you to earlier. He's telling the story of taking dance lessons to prepare for his wedding: "But as you know, ladies, two beautiful women in one room doesn't work. So she only lasted one lesson. To my surprise, my next instructor was even prettier. His name was Chad." In this case, he established that "two beautiful women in one room doesn't work," so the wording is setting up for the next instructor to be a man. As a result, the laugh is not as strong when he finally reveals, "his name is Chad." Here's the version I suggested he try: "But as you know, ladies, two beautiful women in one room doesn't work. Our next instructor was Chad. And he was even prettier ... joke's on her." This version is six words shorter but with the tag/topper of "joke's on her," it includes two solid laughs instead of just one weak laugh.

Remember, any time you spend tweaking jokes and playing with them is a waste until you deliver it to an audience. The audience is the final judge. Did the rearrangement work? My client emailed me the result: "I did the change to Chad joke, and it worked. They loved it!"

4. Are You Leaving the Interpretation up to the Audience?

As I've explained, generating laughs involves the audience's mind. As a speaker, you use words to paint a picture for your audience, so you want to make sure the picture you paint is clear and exactly the picture you want to create. If I say "flower," what picture comes to mind? How about if I say "ice cream"? And what if I say "Think of a color"? Now, if instead of leaving it up to you, the reader, to paint the picture in your mind, what if I get specific? If I say, "Picture a rose," what comes to mind? You picture a rose but the color is still open to interpretation. If I say "red rose" you will picture a red rose. Use details. In fact, "red rose" isn't specific enough; "long-stemmed red rose" is more like it.

5. Is the Twist at the End?

Small adjustments to word order and trying to minimize the words after the joke is revealed can make a big difference in the laugh you get. Consider this example from Rodney Dangerfield: "I played one club that was so tough they had 'broken leg of lamb' on the menu." In this case, "broken leg of lamb" is the twist—actually, "broken" is the twist. So if I was in a position to give feedback on this joke, I would suggest leaving out "on the menu." Or perhaps having "menu" helps, if you arrange the joke a different way: "I played one club that was so tough, on the menu they had 'broken leg of lamb'" or "I played one club that was so tough, they served 'broken leg of lamb.'"

Finally, here's my own example of playing with word order: "I love high heels, and I beg my wife to wear them. She's finally agreed, and this weekend she's going to let me." I really had to work on memorizing the joke exactly this way because whenever I would just do it, the structure wouldn't come out right. Notice that the twist is "me" and that it comes at the very end. Often I would mess it up and say it one of these two ways: "I love high heels and I beg my wife to wear them. She's finally agreed she's going to let me this weekend" or "I love high heels and I beg my wife to let me wear them." Notice that the funniest version is when the twist has the very last word.

6. Is the Surprise Too Far Away?

This Shakespeare quote from *Hamlet* is frequently found in humor and comedy-writing books: "Brevity is the soul of wit." So you can appreciate how difficult the task of being brief can be. Here's a follow up attributed to Mark Twain: "I didn't have time to write a short letter, so I wrote a long one instead." By the way, that quote has been attributed to a large variety of people including Blaise Pascal, Voltaire, and Kim Kardashian. The value of brevity in comedy and humor comes into play when you consider how far the twist is from the key word(s). Author Mel Helitzer provides this example in *Comedy Writing Secrets*: "On the road into town there was a sign in an empty field that said, 'Three miles ahead, lots for sale.' So I went to the location, but to my surprise, there was nothing there."

Notice how far away "nothing there" is from "lots for sale." When the speaker said the words "nothing there," the audience would have to remember that the sign said "lots for sale," make the connection, and conclude it was funny. Helitzer provides this shortened version for consideration: "I saw this sign: 'Lots for sale.' But there was nothing there."[92] The distance between concepts is nice and short. Your audience wouldn't have to struggle to remember exactly what you said.

Now that I've addressed the words you use, let's take a look at some nonverbal issues that could affect the laughs you receive. Having at least an audio recording is essential. Better yet, make a video recording.

7. Did You Talk Over the Laugh?

This question actually refers partly to joke structure and partly to delivery. From a structural standpoint, having the twist at the end of the sentence helps ensure that you won't be talking when the audience wants to laugh. From a delivery standpoint, the question is this: Did you pause long enough for the laugh to develop? When you're expecting a laugh, and it isn't there immediately, your nervousness can heighten and your desire to fill the silence can cause you to move on too quickly with whatever you planned to say next. When it comes to delivering jokes and humorous material, there are two essential pauses. I've already shared the importance of pausing but I'm going to ... pause ... and tell you again.

The first pause comes right before you deliver the twist, allowing your audience enough time to complete the visual and create the assumption or expectation. The second pause comes after you give the twist or drop the punch line. This second pause gives your audience time to complete the little puzzle you created for them. If you start talking, they will stop laughing, even if they haven't started laughing yet. The audience will do this out of respect and because they don't want to miss hearing what you're going to say next. Remember what I said about comedians actually training their audiences not to laugh?

In addition to pausing correctly, consider the following delivery-related questions to help you troubleshoot your joke:

- Did you talk too fast?

- Did you mumble? How well did you enunciate?
- Was there incongruity between your facial language, body language and the words you were saying?
- Was there a noise, distraction, or interruption?
- Could there be a problem for this audience with the target or subtext of the joke?

The Laugh Troubleshooter Process consists of two parts. The first part is the inspection process outlined above. Basically you are trying to locate the potential reasons your joke didn't generate a laugh. The potential reasons fall into two general categories: not enough information or too much information.[93] The audience will be confused if you don't provide enough information. And, as I've already explained, "A confused audience won't laugh." The source of confusion might be the audience could not understand the actual words you spoke, or they didn't understand the references you used. The audience already knows too much, which is the second way you can interfere with a laugh. Maybe they've heard a similar joke before or maybe they are too close to the target of the joke. For example, if you do a joke targeting Ronald Reagan at a Republican convention, you aren't going to get a lot of laughs. So once you've done your inspection and you've identified a potential reason for not getting a good laugh, you can make a correction.

Obviously, if the issue was your delivery, you'll need to work on practicing with the modified delivery. If you experience technical difficulties, like the microphone cutting out or a noise in the environment, the only thing to remember is to stop your delivery and rephrase as needed to make sure the audience has all the information.

The second part of The Laugh Troubleshooter Process is to reconfigure the joke. Earlier in this chapter, I provided several examples of arranging the words to generate the best laugh. The best practice is to rearrange and try again and assess the result of the modified version. Try two or three times to make a joke work. Don't give up too soon.

11.

The Unfortunate Truth—Why You Aren't Funnier

By now you are, hopefully, beginning to realize that being funny is a skill that can be learned and developed. Plus, you are probably wondering, "Since being funny can be taught and learned, why are some people funnier than others?" What is the key to being funnier? Why does it seem we are stuck with the amount of funny we had when we were born? That very question has been studied over and over again. Carol Dweck, the author of *Mindset*, explains that the answer isn't one over the other but that both are constantly in play.[94] How does that apply to being funny? Something happened early on in your life, and you didn't even know it. Or, if you're like me, a lot happened that you didn't know about. On your path to growing up, there was a fork in the road, and you didn't even see it. Don't worry; it's not your fault. No one sees it. That fork in the road was a subtle, subconscious decision. The path to the right was the path to being funny and to continue trying to get laughs. The path to the left lead to being okay with the status quo.

For some people, making others laugh is such a thrill they try to do it every chance they got. Some of these people turn into the class clown and are willing to do anything to get a laugh ("Hey, look, noodles are coming out my nose!"). Others decided to travel more toward "the class wit" route, preferring to use words like a magician uses magic. These individuals enjoyed playing with humor and being funny. As they continued to joke, they became "naturally" funny through implicit learning. And still others, faced with those who were obviously competing to be the funniest person, decided (perhaps subconsciously) that trying to be funny wasn't worth the risk; the reward just wasn't enough. Maybe they even tried on occasion to be funny and missed the mark. Perhaps their friends or family suggested that they weren't funny or couldn't be funny, or worse, suggested that being funny was inappropriate.

Failure is painful, being scolded is painful, and we don't like either one, so we seek to remove ourselves from that discomfort. We decide not to try that again. To compensate and "feel better," our self-talk reinforces the decision to avoid humor and make it seem the right thing to do. After all, "I'm just not funny." Individuals can actually learn (also through implicit learning) how not to be funny. The only difference is a matter of focus.

Let me give you an example from Will Smith. In a *Reader's Digest* interview, he shared how he worked to find jokes that worked with the black kids he hung out with and the white kids he went to school with.

> So I got the best of both worlds. I think that is where my comedy developed. In black neighborhoods, everybody appreciated comedy about real life. In the white community, fantasy was funnier. I started looking for the jokes that were equally hilarious across the board, for totally different reasons.[95]

Do you see that? "I started looking for the jokes that were equally hilarious." He decided being funny was important to him, so he kept working on it. But if he had stopped, like most of us do, he would have encountered ... arrested development. Arrested Development simply means that your ability to be funny reaches a certain level and doesn't develop any more. And we reinforce the level where we stop by saying things like,

"I'm just not funny."

Meanwhile....

You aren't enjoying the same success as funny people. But guess what? You can unblock your arrested humor development and begin learning and practicing how to be funny! Once you can get beyond your arrested development, you'll be challenged by your mindset. The following statements from MindsetOnline.com describe this situation:

> In a fixed mindset, people believe their basic qualities, like their intelligence or talent, are simply fixed traits.
>
> In a growth mindset, people believe that their most basic abilities can be developed through dedication and hard work—brains and talent are just the starting point.[96]

You've probably figured out that I am a big believer in having a growth mindset and I love all the hope that Carol Dweck and her work offer. Mindset, mindset, mindset, I talk a lot about mindset, don't I? Hang in there you are also about to learn about chicken sexing.

How Your "Funny Bone" Develops

Whenever you encounter a "naturally" funny person, you are actually experiencing the result of years of implicit learning. What is implicit learning? Put simply, implicit learning is the type of learning that takes place without awareness that we are, in fact, learning. Implicit learning is passive (like me going to the gym), meaning that people acquire knowledge and understanding through exposure. Because there is no conscious awareness that learning occurred, implicit learning gives what you could describe as intuition. Our brain's number one priority is keeping us alive. As a result, our brains are constantly paying attention, learning, and taking note of what works and what doesn't. In the case of being funny and making others laugh, we observe why others laugh. Then later, we try to recreate the situation that caused laughter.

When we are children and fully eager to learn, the brain can't get enough. After all, our primary job as children is to learn. This type of implicit learning goes into our brain, mostly the basal ganglia and amygdala, and becomes an unconscious talent or intuition. Daniel Goleman, an emotional intelligence expert, explains it this way: "The basal ganglia extracts decision rules: when I did that, that worked well; when I said this, it bombed. Our accumulated life wisdom is stored in this primitive circuitry."[97]

"Naturally funny" people, as young children, develop an intuition about how to be funny by way of observation, trial and error, and trusting what they have implicitly learned. All the while, the brain is recording what has worked, what hasn't worked, the situation and environment, and even the responses from the people involved.

All of this learning is creating a library of experiences stored in implicit memory that a person recalls with little effort. Let's take a closer look at implicit memory.

What is implicit memory? I'm glad you asked.

According to brainhq.com, "Implicit memory is a type of long-term memory that stands in contrast to explicit memory in that it doesn't require conscious thought. It allows you to do things by rote. This memory isn't always easy to verbalize, since it flows effortlessly in our actions."[98]

That's right. We are always learning and storing what we learned in memory. We can recall the information with little effort and can't easily explain how we know it. By the way,

BrainHQ.com is a website and a brain training system based on proven scientific research. If you read articles on the website you'll effortlessly use impressive words like amygdala, basal ganglia, and medulla oblongata. Shout out to *The Waterboy*!

Chicken Sexing, British Aircraft, and Being Funny

David Eagleman, neuroscientist and best-selling author and speaker, gives two examples of how we learn and gain knowledge unconsciously in his book *Incognito*.[99] In the book, he talks first about something called "chicken sexing." Apparently when chickens hatch, people who raise chickens need to separate the males from the females quickly. Doing so is called chicken sexing. Now, there are people in Japan who do it best. Americans haven't figured out how to separate male chickens from female chickens very well. Certainly not the only area on which Americans are falling behind. The problem is that no one who knows how to do it well can really explain how they do it because the technique is based on very small differences that defy verbalization. As a result, chicken sexing is taught by having a novice go through the process while a master chicken sexer observes. After each attempt, the master gives feedback: yes or no. After weeks and weeks of this trial-and-error learning, the novice's brain has learned, unconsciously, at a master level and is now a master too.

These novices learn to do something masterfully without being specifically told what to do, and although they can skillfully complete the task, they can't tell you how to do it. Sounds a lot like being funny, doesn't it?

Eagleman's other example is from World War II and results from the British needing a way to identify and accurately distinguish airplanes due to the ongoing bombings they were experiencing. Now, much like the "natural" chicken sexers, there were some individuals who could differentiate between British planes returning home from German planes on their way to bomb targets.

But, again, the natural plane spotters were unable to explain how they were able to tell the difference between British and German planes. Over time though, the British finally adopted a training routine that involved taking a guess and allowing the expert to give feedback: yes or no. And overtime with practice, the new spotters were able to develop the skill similar to that of their coaches.

But again, they couldn't tell others how to do it. Again, it sounds a lot like making people laugh, doesn't it? Most people believe that you can't teach how to be funny or that being funny can't be learned. The primary reason is that the people who are probably considered to be the funniest people—stand-up comics—can't explain what they do, just like chicken sexing and plane spotting. The best stand-up comics developed through trial and error without having anyone explicitly teach them. And, as we already learned, this type of learning takes a tremendous amount of time. In fact, most comics believe it takes a minimum of 10 years to even begin to know what you're doing. Famous comedian Louis C.K. believes it takes longer. His advice to a young comic:

> Keep in mind that you are in for a looooong haul of ups and downs and nothing and something. It takes at least 15 years, usually more, to make a great comic. Most flame out before they get there.[100]

Now, most comedians still take the grind-it-out trial-and-error approach to writing jokes and being funny. Peter Sims shares that comedian Chris Rock works hard and tests out his material. Here's an excerpt:

His early performances can be painful to watch. Jokes will ramble, he'll lose his train of thought and need to refer to his notes, and some audience members sit with their arms folded, noticeably unimpressed. The audience will laugh about his flops—laughing at him, not with him.[101]

Chris Rock is by no means alone in his approach. In fact, this approach is ubiquitous in comedy. I've been waiting this entire time to use the word ubiquitous. Another bucket list item crossed off!

In a *New York Times* article by Jonah Weiner, Jerry Seinfeld describes his process in the following way:

> I was obsessed with figuring that out. The way I figure it out is I try different things, night after night, and I'll stumble into it at some point, or not. If I love the joke, I'll wait. If it takes me three years, I'll wait.[102]

Fortunately, there is a better way. On the one hand, you still have to practice and test out the material, but you don't have to do it in a vacuum. If you know why people laugh, the elements necessary for a joke and the basic understanding of human laughter, your work gets more focused and productive.

12.

The Safe Humor Solution™

Whenever I was scouring the Internet for every piece of advice I could find on adding humor to a speech, one of the most frequent pieces I found was "be careful; humor is dangerous. You may offend your audience." In fact, several "experts" said that reason alone is enough to not even bother with humor. Inconceivable! All the time I invested working with my coach and all the books I read to get good at being funny lead me to understand two very important traits about humor:
1. Humor is often directed at a target.
2. Humor has something called a subtext.

These two elements combine to form the danger level of humor. Either the target, or the subtext, or both can offend the audience. Let's start by taking a close look at humor having a target.

Target

In the book *Comedy Writing Secrets*, Mel Helitzer describes his recipe for humor and the first essential ingredient is that humor must have a target.[103] My comedy coach, Jerry Corley, says that comedy is a veiled attack.[104] We are attacking someone or something. We are making fun of somebody's misfortune or weakness. We as humans tend to laugh at others but rarely laugh when even the smallest adversity confronts us.

As Mel Brooks explains, "If I got a paper cut, that's a tragedy. If you fell down an open manhole and died, that's comedy." Laughing at someone falling into a manhole is an example of the Superiority Theory of humor first introduced by Aristotle and Plato.[105] Simply put, people laugh when they feel superior. Because jokes often have a target and the audience will laugh when they feel superior, we can review our potential jokes to get a feel for a relativity level of "safety."

As you create jokes, keep these important points in mind regarding the target:
- Know who YOU can joke about.
- Be certain you know who or what your target is.
- Be certain about who your audience is okay joking about.
- If in doubt, make yourself the target. But be careful about that, too.

Know Who YOU Can Joke About

Jerry Corley provides this solution in his book, Breaking Comedy's DNA. There is a rule, however, when you're attacking something or someone other than yourself.

We must remember to attack UP.

What do we mean by "attacking up?" When we say "attack up," that means we can only attack things that we perceive are superior to us, that is, the government, Congress, the police, a teacher, the principal, our boss, or mother-in-law, or someone else who has done us wrong.[106]

In our society, I, as a white male, would need to be very careful performing jokes about women and minorities. In addition to Jerry's list, celebrities are usually "safe" targets. For example, OMGfacts.com has this tidbit on Twitter: "In Texas, it's legal to shoot a Bigfoot on sight." My twist: "Which is why Kim Kardashian doesn't go to Texas." Notice Jerry lists "someone who has done you wrong" as an acceptable target. You can violate the "attack up" rule once you establish the reason and the need to "retaliate."

Be Certain Who Your Target Is

Don't let your audience decide or infer the target of the joke. Remember this Brian Kiley joke?

The other day our boy talked back to my wife. She told him to do something and he said, "No. I don't want to." So I had to pull him aside and say, "Listen, you have to . . . teach me how to do that."

I use that joke a lot as an example of how humor works. In most workshops when I ask the attendees, "Who is the target of that joke?" women typically say the wife, but men typically say the husband. So regardless of the fact that I think Brian is joking about himself, there are some in the audience who believe the wife is the target. Frankly, you don't want that kind of uncertainty. The best way to avoid an uncertain target for your audience is to establish the facts to support the target prior to delivering the joke. Unfortunately clarifying the target will require some testing. For Brian Kiley's joke above, one possible way to clarify that he is the target could be stating "I'm a bit of a pushover" in the setup. But, that's just a possibility. The only way to know if it works is to test it out.

Another piece of advice I offer public speakers about using humor is to "know your audience." I also recommend taking that advice a step farther and deciding who your audience is okay joking about.

Know Who Your Audience Is Okay Joking About

Mel Helitzer clearly states that you won't be successful unless your audience has as much distaste for the target of the joke.[107] You have to make sure your audience feels superior.

One way to do that is just ask. If you're speaking to a corporation, chances are they joke about regulators, competitors, or maybe even the corporate office. If you are speaking at a political dinner, the obvious choice is to poke fun at the "other" party. *In The Message of You*, Judy Carter shares that speaker and author Connie Podesta's approach is to not even make fun of a company's competition because she would like to also speak at that company.[108] Connie provides something to consider seriously. Our humor provides an insight into us as people, so think about your targets and what that might say about you. Unfortunately, this uncertainty about the target of humor can draw the all-too-common-and-easy advice to just use self-deprecating humor.

If in Doubt, Joke about Yourself

"Experts" commonly advise, "If in doubt, make yourself the target." That's good advice in some cases. For example, from an article in Inc.com: "the self-deprecating boss was rated—as a more likable, trustworthy, and caring leader."[109] Use self-deprecating humor to balance out your ego whenever you build yourself up. For instance, if you have just told people how great you are, balance that boast out by taking yourself down a notch or two with some healthy self-deprecation. This will let your audience know you don't take yourself too seriously and that you're likeable.

There are a couple of "gotchas" when it comes to

self-deprecating humor, however. Making yourself the target can work as long as you follow a couple of guidelines. The first guideline is don't joke about your ability related to why you are speaking, though you can joke about the reason you're speaking (your expertise) if it's about your early self and you have overcome the situation.

Here's an example from Joe Polish, marketing superstar:

> Dan said I'm great at taking pictures with famous people. Absolutely I am a total name-dropper and linking myself to credibility. If you don't have any and I certainly don't have any credibility.
>
> That was supposed to be funny by the way; sorta. (Laughter)
>
> Pretend, pretend like it's funny.[110]

At the end of that presentation, Joe is making a pitch and has something to sell. Do you think there's a chance he didn't sell as much as he'd hoped?

The second guideline is to use self-deprecation sparingly, meaning a little bit goes a long way. One study indicated that using too much could hurt your expertise and reliability with your audience.[111] An excellent example of the right amount and the right target is Daniel Pink's Ted Talk:

> In the late 1980s, in a moment of youthful indiscretion, I went to law school.
>
> To put it mildly, I didn't do very well. I, in fact, graduated in the part of my law school class that made the top 90% possible.
>
> I never practiced law a day in my life; I pretty much wasn't allowed to.[112]

His TED Talk is about his motivation research and doesn't depend on his authority as a lawyer so these jokes are okay. However, if they had been about his research ability, they could have created some doubt in the audience's mind.

Here is another great example from Warren Buffett.

> I buy expensive suits. They just look cheap on me.

Notice that Buffet is targeting his looks with self-deprecation. Remember, the first guideline is to stay away from your competence, skill, integrity, and service, especially if you're speaking for your business or in sales. If your audience doesn't know you well, they may actually believe you and question if you are the one to do the job. Ronald Reagan was an expert at disarming his detractors using a little self-deprecation. When his opponent tried to make his age an issue, he began making fun of his age, and he took all their power away.

> Yes, we have a trade deficit, but this isn't entirely new—the United States had a merchandise trade deficit in almost all of the years between 1790 and 1875.
>
> I remember them well.
>
> Of course, I was only a boy at the time.[113]

Now that I've explained the target of a joke and how to successfully understand and know your target, the next element is subtext.

Subtext

Just like music, poetry, and art, humor and jokes can have subtext. Subtext is simply the implicit or metaphorical meaning. I learned a lot about subtext when I read *How to Write Funny: Your Serious, Step-By-Step Blueprint for Creating Incredibly, Irresistibly, Successfully Hilarious Writing* by Scott Dikkers, founder of TheOnion.com. Three things Scott says stand out related to subtext:

> The subtext of any piece of humor writing is a simple statement of opinion.

You can identify subtext by looking closely at a single funny line and asking yourself, "What is this line really saying?"

What you'll find is that once the joke is deconstructed, it's communicating a strong value judgment or opinion held by the writer about life.[114]

Take a look at this joke:

> Gasoline prices are highest in Hawaii, closing in on $4 a gallon. President Bush said, "See, I told you it wasn't only in our country!" David Brenner

First, who is the target? President Bush. Second, what is the subtext? What is this line really saying? That President Bush is an uneducated fool? What is the value judgment? This joke is a good example because David Brenner told the joke; he's revealing how he feels about President Bush. Plus, the same can be said for people who laugh at the joke too; they feel the same way. Now you can see how the target and subtext of humor are the two elements responsible for humor being "dangerous." Here's an example from my life:

> The department manager at AIG said, "My feet are killing me."

> My response, "Any chance they will succeed?"

What is the subtext of this joke? Based on my relationship with this manager, the subtext is easily identified as I secretly wish for her passing. However, I actually just enjoy being funny, and this literal interpretation twist was too easy to pass up. My experience has revealed a couple of truths related to subtext: Nonverbal subtext is a thing, too. Or, as my mother always said, "It's not what you say, but the way you say it." My rule of thumb: "If you wouldn't say the subtext outright, don't joke about it." To avoid the possibility of offending your audience, simply identify the target and the subtext. Taking the few extra minutes to solidify these two elements will make all the difference.

Consider this example when Judy Carter shares a story where an attempt to create a little humor based on the town she was speaking in didn't work out as well as she'd hoped:

> Since I had time the day before, I walked around town with my camera taking pictures of possible tourist attractions. I took a picture of a bait shop, calling it "the freshest sushi in the world." I took a picture of their tattoo parlor and called it an art museum. The slide show got big laughs and I thought it was very successful. Then I checked my email. "Thanks for flying in from L.A. to make fun of our home. It's a better place now that you're not here."[115]

Although many "experts" warn about the dangers of using humor and being offensive, you really don't have to avoid using humor altogether. When you know the target and subtexts of your jokes and your material, you are in the best possible position to keep your audience happily laughing.

13.

Where to Add Humor

The value of humor extends beyond the boundaries of your speech or presentation. Depending on the reason you are speaking, adding humor to the ancillary components of your performance will set the stage, generate interest, and even improve attendance.

Your Bio

Your bio can be one of the most important pieces you write. If people are reading your bio, they're interested in you. Maybe they want to hire you, or maybe they are coming to hear you speak. Whatever the reason, your bio will either get them excited or turn them off. A brag-fest bio, like a "look at me" introduction, will turn them off. Adding a bit of humor to take yourself down a notch will allow you to endear yourself to the reader and have them on your side. In short, adding humor to your bio will humanize you, despite your accomplishments, and make you more relatable.

Your Speech Title

The title of your speech will appear in writing in the program or marketing material and will also likely be spoken by the person introducing you. Either way, your audience will be making decisions based on the title of your speech or presentation. In addition to describing the subject, the title can and should attract attention, as well as set the mood for the audience. When I won the District 3 Humorous Speech contest, the title of my speech was, "The Day I Rode My Bicycle 100 Miles ... by Mistake." That title ensured I took the stage with the audience already laughing.

Your Introduction

Chances are, you've already written your introduction. Does it have humor in it? It should. Just to be clear, your introduction is not your opening remarks, and it's not your bio. Nope, your introduction is the piece presented to the audience by the Master of Ceremonies. Thanks to Fred E. Miller, author of *No Sweat Public Speaking*, for that clarification! Mr. Miller continues by explaining that an introduction should answer three questions:

1. Why this subject?
2. Why this speaker?
3. Why now?[116]

The "why this speaker" section is the perfect place to add a little bit of self-deprecating humor. Here's an example from Hall of Fame Speaker Joel Weldon:

> You'll hear what happened and how that young man, now an old guy ... yes, he is old! I found out his Social Security number is 5 ... and that he sat next to Benjamin Franklin in kindergarten!

That touch of humor lowers resistance from the audience and the self-deprecating humor will help put your audience at ease. Some introductions leave the audience with a bit of ill will toward the speaker. Most people know the speaker probably wrote the introduction, and if you come across as full of yourself or a bit pompous, you're going to have to work harder to get the audience on your side. Fred Miller provides his introduction as an excellent example of fun and not too serious:

> I did a little research and discovered our guest speaker had been in the Coffee Service business for many years.
>
> Since he used to sell Coffee, I asked him to "PERK UP" our meeting, and not let it become a "GRIND."
>
> I've been told he "ESPRESSOS" himself well, and would never be considered a "DRIP."
>
> I don't want to "SPILL THE BEANS" on his talk, and I'm curious, as I'm sure you are, to see and hear what he's "BREWED UP" for us.[117]

Your Opening Remarks

As you take the stage, what has happened up to this point doesn't matter. The only thing that matters is your next comments. The audience is paying the most attention at this point. And they might be paying attention only to decide if they are going to keep paying attention. As he takes the stage, Fred Miller turns to the master of ceremonies and says, "Great introduction. Thanks a latte." He wrote his introduction in a way that setup this humorous opening remark. Nice touch. Below are some additional examples of humor being used effectively to open a speech.

The beginning is the most important part of the work.
Plato

Ronald Reagan loved to use humor in his opening remarks. Here is an example from a White House Reception for the National Association of Elementary School Principals and the National Association of Secondary School Principals.

Well, thank you all, and let me welcome you all to the White House. You know, I've been out of school for a little over 50 years now, but I still get nervous around so many principals. [Laughter][118]

The March 1957 edition of *Boys' Life* includes this account. Introducing the late Thomas A. Edison at a dinner, the toastmaster mentioned his many inventions, dwelling at length on the talking machine. The old inventor said gently, "I thank the gentleman for his kind remarks but I must insist upon a correction. God invented the talking machine. I only invented the first one that can be shut off.[119]

During the "Finding, Creating & Delivering a World-Class Speech" teleseminar on SpeakerMatch.com, Patrick Snow shared how he likes to open a speech by commenting on his introduction: "Thank you for reading that introduction. That could very well be the best introduction that I've ever written. Yes, I wrote that introduction and it's the best one that I've ever written." Patrick continues:

It always gets a 5, 7, 10 second eruption in laughter. They love it because now they know you aren't some big egomaniac, some crazy speaker, that's a narcissist or whatever else. They see your humor right out of the gate. After that 7 to 10 seconds of laughter I come back with ... "and that's the only joke I'm going to tell today." And then I get another 2 to 3 seconds of laughter.[120]

How much humor should you use at the beginning of your presentation? Well, it depends. Steve Rizzo is a Hall of Fame motivational business speaker who uses a lot of humor. On his website, www.steverizzo.com, Steve shares his approach:

> No matter what group I'm speaking to or what program I'm giving, I always start off with 5 to 10 minutes of non-stop comedy. Why? Because nothing can captivate an audience and hold their attention more than "The Power of Laughter." As soon as the laughter starts I can actually feel the tension in the room dissipate. Their energy level is cranked and everyone is primed for a good time and a great learning experience.[121]

You should know, however, that Steve used to be a headlining comedian, so don't feel obligated to match his approach. But do consider crafting some laugh points into your opening remarks.

Your Stories and Anecdotes

Story seems to be the "holy grail" of recommended speech techniques and perhaps with good reason. In the book *Wired for Story: The Writer's Guide to Using Brain Science to Hook Readers from the Very First Sentence*, Lisa Cron states,

> Story is what makes us human, not just metaphorically but literally. Recent breakthroughs in neuroscience reveal that our brain is hardwired to respond to story; the pleasure we derive from a tale well told is nature's way of seducing us into paying attention to it.[122]

Telling humorous stories and anecdotes is one of the most common recommendations for adding humor to a speech. However, what *is* a funny story? What is humorous? I'm reminded of the movie Kung Fu Panda where Oogway goes to tell Shifu that he has some bad news. Shifu responds that there is just news and there is no such thing as good news or bad news.

Why am I reminded of this? Simple. A story is just a story until you make it funny or humorous. What then makes a story funny? My speech about the day I rode my bicycle 100 miles could be either a drama or a tragedy. It makes people laugh because, in reality, we tend to laugh at other people's challenges.

The stories that will get you the most laughs are the ones that have conflict. When I started taking improv classes, I learned that comedy, as I previously shared, is trying to get from point A to point B and encountering obstacles. In short, obstacles equal conflict. You can use the Laugh Generator Process to add humor to a story—any story. You will get bigger laughs if that story is about you encountering obstacles. A funny story starts with a bad situation. In my story, the bad situation started at the beginning of the bicycle ride and got worse when my friend, who assured me he would lead the way, missed the turn. And then it got even worse from there.

Your Closing

Typically, your closing remarks or call to action will be what "sticks" with your audience. What is your call to action? It's what you're going to encourage them to do or start to do. Regardless, make sure you've added some laughs to ensure your audience has the best chance to take action. Speaking coaches often recommend writing the ending first. That is probably good advice. Whatever amount of time you have with your audience, that time will eventually come to a close. Because you know there's going to be a "break up," you may as well plan for it.

> *Laughter is not at all a bad beginning for a friendship, and it is far the best ending for one.*
> **Oscar Wilde**

Performance artist Marina Abramovic cautions, "People put so much effort into starting a relationship and so little effort into ending one." Consider how you will end your relationship with your audience. Will you be taking questions after your presentation? If so, you should consider crafting a second closing.

How Much Humor?

It's a common question: "How much humor do I need?" Or sometimes speakers ask the question this way: "What percentage of my presentation should be humor?" The first answer is to think in terms of laughs per minute, rather than percentage, because percentage is hard to measure. Laughs per minute is a common term in comedy and it suits our need nicely. Consider the example I shared in the introduction of Sir Ken Robinson's TED Talk. A *Business Insider* article shared that Sir Ken Robinson's TED Talk had two laughs a minute, whereas the movie *Anchor Man* had only 1.6 laughs per minute and *The Hangover* had 2.5 laughs per minute.[123]

Two laughs a minute—that was in the first five minutes of his speech. You may want to do the same and get several laughs in the first minutes of your presentation. From there, you can vary the frequency and density of laughs. But keep in mind Zig Ziglar's plan: "Every 7 to 9 minutes—you can set your watch—I'm going to lay a funny on you."[124] Several opportunities exist for you to add humor, and they extend beyond your speech or even your time on stage. As you approach your engagement, consider all the opportunities you have to interact with your audience. Every one of them is an opportunity to provide some humor and generate a laugh.

14.

The Material Machine™: Finding More Humorous Content

Where does humorous material come from? These are my favorite places to find content that generates laughs: ad-libs, audience interaction, the event, the event location, the speech, related quotes and clichés, stories, your life, daily events, your audience, time of the year, and current media.

Ad-Libs

There are two types of ad-libs. The one you prepared and the one you didn't. The best way to ad-lib is with preparation. It's true. Although most comedians act as if everything is happening in the moment, their material is often practiced beforehand. John Cantu observed this practice in a conversation he had with Gene Perrett. Apparently Gene was performing and had been opening for Sammy Davis Jr. The audience would leave the show exclaiming what a great ad-libber Sammy was.

> *The best ad-libs are the ones that have been written down.*
> **George Burns**

But, Gene knew the truth and told John Cantu that Sammy ad-libbed the same spot, the same way every performance.[125]
    Comedians typically prepare some "savers" in case a joke

falls flat and gets no laughs. As a speaker, you can do the same thing. In fact, you can write some humor for all sorts of unexpected events. Remember, your audience is in the same frame of mind as the speaker. If any issue gets to you and you start having a bad time, your audience will start having a bad time too. Take, for example, the following possible problems:

- Your microphone quits.
- Your microphone pops.
- The event next door disrupts you.
- You trip on your way up to the stage or on the stage or off the stage.
- The room is too hot or too cold.
- The lights in the room go out.

Here's some great advice and an example from Alan Weiss, author of *Million Dollar Speaking: The Professional's Guide to Building Your Platform*:

> Never use ad-lib humor to degrade anyone else individually. Use it to mock a situation so that you're never seen as picking on anyone.
>
> When I keynoted for Toyota Financial one year, I heard a great deal of good-natured banter during the introduction about the discomfort of being in Phoenix in July, where it must have been 114 degrees in the shade. When I walked on stage, I deadpanned: "I know why you're here, it's not surprising. The surface of the sun was already booked." After that, whatever I said was golden.[126]

To ad-lib, make a list of anything and everything that can happen during a presentation. Here is my list. Go ahead and add to it.

- The host mispronounces your name
- Host gets your bio wrong

- Host gets your intro wrong
- Event running long, your time is cut
- You forget your place
- You make a verbal mistake
- You trip
- You trip AND fall
- You mumble
- You drop something
- You spill water
- Microphone doesn't work
- Microphone quits working
- Microphone making noise; crackle, pop, hiss, etc.
- Microphone makes noise intermittently
- Computer not working
- Computer works but then stops
- No slides
- Wrong slides
- Slide with misspelling
- Projector quits
- Projector won't work
- No handouts
- Wrong handouts
- Not enough handouts
- Lights go out
- Lights go off and on intermittently
- Door opens
- Door opens repeatedly
- Knocking on the door
- Room is noisy
- AC/Heater make noise
- Sudden loud noise
- Fire alarm

- Fire drill
- Room too hot
- Room too cold
- Audience is noisy
- Audience distracted
- Audience talking
- Audience (lots of empty seats)
- Audience (someone continually coughs)
- Q&A section
- Question you didn't expect
- Inappropriate question
- Only one person asking questions

From The Laugh Generator Process, consider upside/downside and who, what, when, where, why, and how to come up with humorous things you could say for anything that might happen during your speeches or presentations.

Audience Interaction

If you are building audience interaction into your presentation, you are also building in the opportunity for humor. Last month, I was listening to a speaker who interacted with the audience by asking a lot of questions. However, the questions he was asking were somewhat generic and didn't always elicit the answer he wanted. In this case, his reply implied that we, the audience, weren't really getting it or paying attention. However, with a little preparation, he could have handled our confusion better and included some humor.

Here is Laurie Guest, CSP, talking about Billy Riggs in her ebook: "As a performer, Billy was quick witted and played off everything the volunteers did.... I'm sure he has used most of his lines many times, but he gave the illusion that they were impromptu, and that rocked." [127]

If you are asking the audience a question to interact with them, make a list of every potential answer you could hear. I know there is the answer you want, but what if the audience doesn't give you that answer? Plan for those other answers and how you can respond in a humorous way that doesn't put down the audience.

The Event

Often times you can create some ad-lib type humor based on what has happened at the event. Here is Alan Weiss with a great example: "I found that one participant, in a prior session, had actually gone onto the stage to draw a picture of his point. I began my speech by introducing myself and then asking if I could just turn my segment over to Joe, as I pulled an easel forward."[128] World Champion Darren LaCroix's *Stage Time* also provided insight on this topic in his newsletter. This particular email caught my attention because the subject line read, "I Just Made a Rookie Mistake." Darren shared the following story:

> When I arrive at any event, I usually look around and listen to the buzz around the room to see if I can customize some humor or points for that specific audience....
>
> I made a rookie mistake, however, by taking a jab at the hotel. I called it a Holiday Inn that had been renovated into a Crowne Plaza. It got some laughs and even some moans. I think I may have even followed up with something worse. It was in poor taste, and I went a bit too far.
>
> I really admire Darren's willingness to call himself out on

the put-down mistake and to share an important lesson he learned about going too far. You can practice creating this type of ad-lib about an event by paying attention when you are at a store or somewhere else in life where you are free to try it and mess up. Toastmasters is also a great opportunity to play with and practice ad-libbing.

The Event Location

Where is the event being held? Which city? You can Google (sensing a trend?) the city and begin gathering facts about the location. Here's an example of using the process of gathering facts about the city of Amarillo, Texas, and creating some customized humor for the audience where I would be speaking. I used these facts to create five minutes of customized humor. In addition to Wikipedia, I gathered facts from several websites. Here are some of the facts I gathered about Amarillo:

- Oprah Winfrey was unsuccessfully sued by local cattlemen for slandering beef.
- The statement that got Oprah sued? "It has just stopped me cold from eating another burger!"
- In order to attend the trial in Amarillo, she relocated her show to Amarillo.
- The city was once the self-proclaimed "Helium Capital of the World" for having one of the country's most productive helium fields.
- Almost a third of the earth's helium supply is stored outside of Amarillo. Helium is a colorless, odorless gas that is totally unreactive.
- Amarillo is known for being cold and windy and the tourism-related websites prefer to dodge the question and not give a straight answer.

- According to the Weather Channel, Amarillo is the windiest city in the US.
- Amarillo is rated nationally as having some of the cleanest air in the country.
- Amarillo is home to attractions like the Cadillac Ranch and the Big Texan Steak Ranch.
- The Big Texan Steak Ranch is home to the 72-ounce steak challenge.
- If you take the challenge and win, in addition to 4.5 pounds of free meat, you receive a t-shirt, a souvenir plastic boot mug, and a certificate of achievement.
- Half of the women who attempt the challenge, do it, but only 1 out of 7 men are able to do it.
- Amarillo is home to Palo Duro Canyon, the second largest canyon in the US.
- The Texas state verb is "fixin' to." There's really nothing to fix, though this Texas saying means that you're about to do something. An example would be, "I'm fixin' to leave."
- Texans also say "all git-out." This means to a great degree, exceedingly, or as much as possible. "She was happier'n all git-out!"
- Texans never ask for a soda, soft drink, or pop. It's Coke—no matter what kind of carbonated refreshment they want.

From here I took these facts and free-associated them. Next, I took each fact through The Laugh Generator Process so that I could identify potential laugh points.

- Oprah Winfrey was unsuccessfully sued by local cattlemen for slandering beef. Apparently in Texas you don't slander beef, you slather it … in gravy.
- The statement that got Oprah sued? "It has just stopped me cold from eating another burger!"

- I know I'm not one to talk, but based on what we know about Oprah's dieting history, she's probably still eating burgers.
- In order to attend the trial in Amarillo, she relocated her show to Amarillo. Yep, she announced on her show ... "You get to go to Amarillo, you get to go to Amarillo, you get to go to Amarillo!"
- The city was once the self-proclaimed "Helium Capital of the World" for having one of the country's most productive helium fields. Apparently in Amarillo, helium grows in fields.
- Almost a third of the earth's Helium supply is stored outside of Amarillo. As you know, helium is a colorless, odorless gas that is totally unreactive. Until you breathe it, and then it's hilarious.
- The second thing I want to know when visiting a new city is what is the weather like? Luckily, I found this in the FAQ section of the Visit Amarillo website.
- Is it true that it's always cold and that the wind blows constantly?
- Our area of Texas does have four seasons. However, our winters are overrated and our summers underrated. Yes, it does snow occasionally, but it usually melts within a few days. In the summer, temperatures climb into the 90s, but the evenings are cool and comfortable. Overall, our city receives 270 days of sunshine per year.
- Notice there was no answer to does the wind blow constantly? Would you like to know why? This is why. According to the Weather Channel, Amarillo is the windiest city in the U.S. Turns out Chicago isn't the Windy City. It's a lie.
- But, there is an upside. Thanks to all that wind, Amarillo

is rated nationally as having some of the cleanest air in the country. Got trash? Just throw it up and let the wind do the rest.
- Once I find out what the weather is like, I take a look at some of the things to do and see.
- Amarillo is home to attractions like the Cadillac Ranch and the Big Texan Steak Ranch. While you can get a steak at the Big Texan Steak ranch, you can't get a Cadillac at Cadillac Ranch.
- The Big Texan Steak Ranch is home to the 72-ounce steak and the 72-hour bypass. I'm sure that is not a coincidence.
- If you take the challenge and win, in addition to 4.5 pounds of free meat, you receive a t-shirt, a souvenir plastic boot mug, and clogged arteries.
- One fact I did find interesting is that half of women who attempt it, do it, but only 1 out of 7 men. Which proves just one thing. Men aren't good at finishing ... anything.
- A 72-ounce steak? Just goes to show you: Everything is bigger in Texas. Yes, except for the canyons. While Arizona is home to the Grand Canyon, Amarillo is home to the canyon not so grande otherwise known as Palo Duro Canyon, the second largest canyon in the US.

Finally, I like to find out some manners and customs to help me blend in with the locals.
- Since it's Texas, I've got my work cut out for me. It's hard to speak Texan. Even Texas Natives have a hard time. Just ask former President George W. Bush.
- Thanks to Coldwell Banker's website, I now know what it means to talk Texan. The Texas state verb is "fixin' to."

There's really nothing to fix, though. This Texas saying means that you're about to do something. Example: "I'm fixin' to leave."
- All git-out. This means to a great degree, exceedingly, or as much as possible. As in: "She was happier'n all git-out!
- If I order a coke, I will be asked, what kind? That's right, Texans never ask for a soda, soft drink, or pop. It's Coke—no matter what kind of carbonated refreshment they want.

And then, of course, I followed my own advice: I recorded my presentation and analyzed it afterwards. Go to chapter 16 when you're ready for those insider tidbits.

The Speech

Your speech itself and the content is the perfect source of humor. In fact, The Laugh Generator Process is designed to find and generate the laughs you're missing out on every time you speak.

Related Quotes and Clichés

What is the theme of your talk? What points are you making? Go to Google and type in "top _____ quotes" and check out some of the quotes. For example, I typed in "top customer service quotes" and found this one: Benjamin Franklin said, "Well done is better than well said." Here is my initial thought for generating a laugh: "All I can say is 'Well said, Mr. Franklin, well said.' Maybe that should be 'Well done, Mr. Franklin, well done.'"

Another quote on customer service from Bill Gates: "Your

most unhappy customers are your greatest source of learning." Use The Laugh Generator Process and the context of your speech to generate some possible laugh lines. I did some additional searches on Bill Gates to get my mind going and came up with these possible laugh lines:
1. Bill would know; I don't think anyone's had more unhappy customers.
2. Think of the lessons they learned just from Windows 10.
3. I can only imagine what they learned from Rover, Bob, and Clippy.
4. Of course, in 2004, Bill also said, "Two years from now, spam will be solved."
5. And your greatest source of $80 Billion.

If this idea really resonates with you, then you can use The Simple Joke Writing System and make two lists. For the Bill Gates quote, I would make one list on "customer service/unhappy customers" and another list on "Bill Gates/Microsoft."

Stories Related to the Themes and Points of Your Speech

I have a keynote speech called "Rolling with Change" where I address strategies for excelling when the unexpected happens, and we are forced to adapt. Often I open that speech by telling them my story of riding 100 miles on my bicycle by mistake. In addition to that personal story, I talk about the Kodak® Company's story and how they didn't successfully deal with change. I share the story of a lady who called 911 three times because McDonald's was out of Chicken McNuggets®. Plus, I share the New Coke® story but include the real stories of how people handled the change by stockpiling the "old" Coke®. Regardless of the point you're trying to make, there are stories that will tie to those points. You generate laughs from those stories using the tools in this book.

Your Life

Much like my story of riding a bicycle 100 miles, you have your stories. Your personal stories provide a powerful way to connect with your audience and get them laughing. How do you know which stories to pick? You pick the stories where you metaphorically have fallen into a manhole. The stories where you encountered obstacles while trying to achieve something will provide for both comedy and learning. When I attended the Dale Carnegie Course, I took specific lessons on these "defining moments" of our lives. A defining moment is a point in time where your character is forged on the fires of fortune or misfortune. I hadn't given them a lot of thought in the past, but these are the perfect stories to include. You're prepared right now to share at least a dozen stories that no one else anywhere has experienced except you. What are these stories? I don't know. But you do.

So carry a notebook or your smartphone with you and begin to note the experiences of your life. Then, one by one, run your life stories through The Laugh Generator Process and add humor. Remember, you aren't creating a documentary. You're creating humor, so get the facts, distort them, and get laughs! To make your life stories funny, write a list of every event, moment, or story in your life. The point or emotion of each event is what makes it memorable. As a result, if you remember it, chances are it will resonate with an audience. Once you have your list of events. Pick one, tell the story, and walk it through

The Laugh Generator Process to find the natural laugh points. Do the same for each story or event.

Daily Events

Every new is day filled with the raw material to create something funny. Just now I was filling gas and noticed a sign on the pump that said, "Each gallon of gasoline contains the following taxes," so I wrote that in my notebook. I included the note about why that caught my attention. Because I am very literally minded, I notice signs like this all the time. Technically the sign should read, "The price of each gallon of gasoline contains the following taxes." I don't know when I will use that note, but because I wrote it down, I will have it when I need it. Keep your notebook handy and record the events that catch your attention. If the event catches your attention, it will catch the attention of your audience too.

Your Audience

You're probably already doing research about your audience, correct? If not, start. Not only will it help make everything about your presentation better, but your humor and jokes will be better too. Here is Laurie Guest, CSP, talking about David Glickman, CSP, in her ebook: "David is a hard act to follow because he customizes the heck out of his content. Not only had he written songs specific to this industry, he was so accurate in his comedic bits that people around me kept saying, "How does he know that? It's like he works with us!"[129]

What does your audience joke about? You should ask them. And while you are asking them, ask them about their major competition. If you know who their competition is, you know who you can probably joke about. But, recall the story I shared in The Safe Humor Solution chapter; not all speakers like to poke fun at a company's competition, and that makes sense unless you want to limit your opportunities. Definitely weigh up the pros and cons as to whether or not to criticize the competition using humor.

Sometimes, though, your audience will actually "let you in on" an existing joke within the organization.

Alan Weiss gives this advice: "Talk to the client in advance and find out something that you can safely use that the group would find funny. For example, there's usually a story about a golf outing, a trip, a sales meeting, a retirement, or some other company legend that can be incorporated."[130]

Current Media

The news and current events can be a tremendous source of humorous material for you. Listening to the radio today, I heard a story that caught my attention. Apparently a rail company in London blamed delays on "strong sunlight." And you think you're having a bad day? I often use the story of an Arizona couple who called 911 when McDonald's failed to include hash browns in their order. My keynotes are related to dealing with and successfully navigating change and the unexpected. Obviously, this couple did not have a healthy skill set for change and dealing with the unexpected.

To use current media, check the trending news stories for the day. Make a note of the ones that catch your attention. Recently, two headlines caught my eye: "Thieves Steal Cheese Worth $160,000" and "George Clooney Talks 25-Minute Proposal." With each headline, read the story. You may have to read several versions of the story. Identify if there is a point within the story you can tie to the point of your presentation or speech. If so, use The Simple Joke Writing System". Then consider doing an incongruity exercise with the time of the year. For example, you'll find out (below) that February is National Hot Breakfast Month. A few weeks ago, I saw this headline: "Woman Reportedly Assaults Waitress over $4 'All-You-Can-Eat' Denny's Pancakes." If you combined National Hot Breakfast Month with this headline about a woman assaulting a waitress over Denny's pancakes, you have a great opportunity for generating some laughs.

Time of the Year

When is your speaking engagement? What month and day? I know you know this, but you probably haven't considered the time of year as a source of some humorous content. But keep in mind, every month is "National _____ Month" and every day is probably "National _____ Day." You can use these observance months and days as starters for humorous content. Bring up an Internet search engine, type in "national days," and hit return. Your search will result in a list of several websites that offer lists of links to national observance days. I picked www.nationaldaycalendar.com.

When I selected February, I got four options. I selected "February Monthly Observations" and got the following list:
- American Heart Month
- An Affair to Remember Month
- Black History Month
- Canned Food Month
- Creative Romance Month
- Great American Pie Month
- National Bake for Family Fun Month

- National Bird Feeding Month
- National Cherry Month
- National Children's Dental Health Month
- National Grapefruit Month
- National Heart Month
- National Hot Breakfast Month
- National Library Lovers Month
- National Macadamia Nut Month
- National North American Inclusion Month
- National Snack Food Month
- National Weddings Month

Next, I entered "official list of national days" and picked this link: all-funny.info/real-list-of-national-days. Going to February, I found out the following:

- February 1 is Serpent Day
- February 2 is Purification Day
- February 3 is Cordova Ice Worm Day
- February 4 is Create A Vacuum Day
- February 5 is Disaster Day
- February 6 is Lame Duck Day
- February 7 is Charles Dickens Day
- February 8 is Kite Flying Day
- February 9 is Toothache Day
- February 10 is Umbrella Day
- February 11 is White T-Shirt Day and Don't Cry Over Spilled Milk Day
- February 12 is National Plum Pudding Day
- February 13 is Get A Different Name Day and Dream Your Sweet Day
- February 14 is Ferris Wheel Day and National Heart to Heart Day
- February 15 is National Gumdrop Day

- February 16 is Do A Grouch A Favor Day
- February 17 is Champion Crab Races Day
- February 18 is National Battery Day
- February 19 is National Chocolate Mint Day
- February 20 is Hoodie Hood Day
- February 21 is Card Reading Day
- February 22 is Be Humble Day
- February 23 is International Dog Biscuit Appreciation Day
- February 24 is National Tortilla Chip Day
- February 25 is Pistol Patent Day (Samuel Colt)
- February 26 is National Pistachio Day
- February 27 is International Polar Bear Day
- February 28 is Public Sleeping Day
- February 29 is National Surf and Turf Day

On which day will you be speaking? Use The Simple Joke Writing System and make two lists. One list will be everything you can think of for the monthly observation and the second list will be everything you can think of for the national day.

Let's recap.

The Material Machine is a checklist to help trigger the many humorous material opportunities around you every day. Here they all are again for you in one quick list:

- Ad-libs
- Audience Interaction
- The Event
- The Event Location
- The Speech
- Stories
- Your Life
- Daily Events
- Your Audience

- Current Media
- Time of Year

16.

Putting it All Together

You now have all the knowledge and processes necessary to generate as many laughs as you'd like. In fact, you now have a complete toolkit. The Public Speaker's Humor Toolkit is made up of tools to help you generate laughs, troubleshoot the laughs that aren't working, turn one laugh into more laughs, and ensure each laugh is as long as possible.

Here's a list of all the tools:
- The Laugh Generator™
- The Simple Joke Writing System™
- The Laugh Multiplier™
- The Laugh Amplifier™
- The Laugh Troubleshooter™
- The Safe Humor Solution™
- The Material Machine™
- The Writer's Block Eradicator™

To get started, I recommend you begin with your current speech or presentation. If you want more laughs, take your speech through The Laugh Generator . If you are already getting some laughs, then use The Laugh Amplifier and The Laugh Multiplier. If you've got places where the laugh works sometimes and not others, then take a look at The Laugh Troubleshooter. Are you worried that you may offend your audience? The Safe Humor Solution will help you analyze each joke and identify two specific elements that could offend your audience. Finally, if you're looking for more humorous content to add to or enhance your presentation, you can use

The Material Machine to help you out. And if you're frustrated and stuck, use The Writer's Block Eradicator.

You can use each tool based on your current need.

But there's a certain magic that happens when the tools are combined and orchestrated to help you be a more humorous speaker. Let's walk through a scenario. Using The Material Machine to find more humorous content, you have an opportunity to enhance every presentation with some humor based on the event location. You can revisit how I created a structured presentation and generated potential laugh points using The Laugh Generator Process when I gave the presentation about Amarillo, Texas. That's in chapter 14.

So now you know my *potential* laugh points. I say potential , because I really don't know if they are funny until I say the line and a real audience laughs. I had the opportunity to present to an Ahwatukee, Arizona Chamber of Commerce group, so I decided to tell them about Amarillo, Texas, and test out the material I generated. What follows is the transcript, which includes where the audience laughed.

I'm ready. (laugh)

I'm sorry. You don't get to interrupt. How many of you are native to the Valley? Exactly, the rest of you moved here from somewhere else. I moved here from Amarillo, Texas. Now, how many of you have heard of Amarillo, Texas or else you've never heard of Amarillo, Texas? (laugh)

How many of you, man in black, are never going to raise your hand no matter what I ask you to do? (laugh) Uh....

Exactly, I'm here to tell you about Amarillo, Texas, because chances are you've driven through it as fast as you could at three in the morning or else you have no intention of going there. In which case, I'll save you a lot of trouble.

I'm going to give you exactly what you need to know about Amarillo.

Amarillo, you may recall, was where Oprah Winfrey was sued for defamation of beef. (laugh)

The local cattle feeders sued her because she said, "It just stopped me cold from ever eating another hamburger." Really, Oprah? I know I'm not one to judge, but I, I'm pretty, I'm pretty sure she's back on the burger wagon. (laugh)

They sued Oprah; they didn't win, but during that trial, they had to move the entire Oprah Winfrey Show to Amarillo from Chicago. I remember the day. I was watching the Oprah show and she said, "You're going to Amarillo, and you're going to Amarillo, and you're going to Amarillo!" And they said, "No, not Amarillo." Going to Amarillo. The city, Amarillo, is the self-proclaimed helium capital of the world. (laugh)

I'll take the, I'll take the laugh, that wasn't even a joke. (laugh)

Amarillo has abundant supply of helium in the helium fields around Amarillo and that is what Wikipedia said, called them, "the helium fields of Amarillo," because that's exactly how helium grows. In fields. Outside of Amarillo is a storage, underground store, natural underground storage container that holds over two-thirds of the nation's helium supply. Now, helium, as you know, is colorless, odorless and unreactive until you breathe it and talk. (laugh)

Then it's hilarious. (laugh)

Right? Who knows what I'm talking about? I went to the Visit Amarillo website to find out a little bit more about Amarillo, and there was this question: "Is it true it is cold and constantly windy there?" And I'm going to read you their answer verbatim. Remember the question is, "Is it cold and constantly windy?" "Our area of Texas does have four seasons," I'm going to put on my best Chamber of Commerce voice. "Our area of Texas does have four seasons. Our winters are overrated and our summers are underrated. We have snow occasionally, but it melts within hours. In the summer, temperatures climb to the nineties, but the evenings are a cool, comfortable, enjoyable seventy-five. Overall, our city receives two hundred days of sunshine per year." The question, "Is it cold and does the wind blow constantly?" They did not answer that question because, yes, the wind blows constantly. (laugh)

Three hundred and sixty-five days of wind. The average wind speed is thirteen miles per hour. The weather channel has named Amarillo the windiest city in the nation. Chicago, you're a fraud. (laugh)

There is an upside, though. Amarillo is nationally ranked for some of the cleanest air in the country. Thanks to the wind. (laugh)

You got trash? Throw it up. (laugh)

Enjoy the trash, Oklahoma. (laugh)

Put that on the Chamber website. (laugh)

Now that you know what the weather is like and a few of the key points about Amarillo, I'm going to share some of the things that you'll want to make sure and see. Amarillo is home to The Big Texan Steak Ranch and the Cadillac Ranch. Interestingly enough, you can get a steak at The Big Texan Steak Ranch, but you can't get a Cadillac at the Cadillac Ranch. (laugh)

Big Texan is home to the seventy-two ounce steak and the seventy-two hour bypass. (laugh)

If you choose to take on the challenge, in addition to four and a half pounds of free beef, you will receive a t shirt, a souvenir plastic mug, and clogged arteries. (laugh)

One fact I do find interesting is that half of the women who compete in the challenge complete it, but only one in seven men. Which just proves what everybody knows; men are horrible at finishing anything. (laugh)

Finally, I want to help you understand the culture, so you can fit in a little bit better. It's Texas, so people speak Texan. For example, the cattle feeders who sued Oprah for slandering beef, because in Texas you don't slander beef, Pa. No, you slather it. (laugh)

Great. Thanks to the Coldwell Banker website, you have some tips on how to speak Texan. The state verb is "fixin' to." (laugh)

And, (laugh)

there's really nothing to fix; it's just that; it means I'm about to do something. Like, Rick is fixin' to wrap up this speech. (laugh)

The other thing you're going to hear a lot of is, "All git-out." (laugh)

It means, "to great degree, exceedingly or as much as possible." Rick's speech was funnier than all git-out. (laugh)

If you don't believe that, well then, get out. (laugh)

And if you order a Coke, just be prepared. You will be asked, "What kind?" Because they don't say soda, they don't say pop, they ask for Coke, regardless of what type of carbonated beverage you want. So now that you know about Amarillo, you understand why I moved from Amarillo. (laugh)

And I hope that I can avoid a disaster for you as well or for y'all, too. (laugh)

In less than 7 minutes I was able to generate 28 laughs, which averages out to 4 laughs a minute. Not too bad.

What follows are my notes looking at and listening to the presentation from The Laugh Troubleshooter Process and The Laugh Amplifier Process. The numbers will match the specific laugh point I'm making a note about.

4. Missed saying the line about slandering beef—"in Texas you don't slander beef, you slather it ... in gravy." Still need to try it.

6. Didn't give the audience time to laugh after last "You're going to Amarillo." Also, really didn't deliver the line quite right; try it again. Didn't give audience time to laugh after, "No, not Amarillo."

8. Didn't emphasize "helium fields" and didn't give time to laugh. Try it again the way I originally wrote it.

11. After 13 miles per hour, try a line like "the average wind speed is faster than a Vespa scooter." Chicago, you're a fraud (Ad-lib, keep it).

12-15. Act-out worked well, delivery fine. Make sure and keep all of it. Most audiences won't get the chamber reference since this group was from the Chamber of Commerce.

20. The "slather" line worked okay here. Missed the opportunity to add the tag/topper "in gravy." Try it as originally written and compare.

22. Stepped on the laugh. Give it more time the next time.

26. Ad-lib worked well, keep it.

28. "Ya'll" ad-lib worked will, keep it.

In this real example, you see most of the Humorous Speaker Toolkit in action. Starting with The Material Machine,

I picked Amarillo, Texas for the event location. The Writer's Block Eradicator tells me not to worry about what is funny and to start gathering facts. So that's what I did. Using the Web, I searched for Amarillo and gathered a bunch of facts that I found interesting. From there, I organized them into a logical order and using concepts from The Laugh Generator Process, with a little help from The Laugh Multiplier, I created some potential laugh points. Specifically, the lines about the wind provided the perfect opportunity to act out "getting rid of the trash" by using the wind. And that line worked out nicely. Finally, after really delivering the speech, recording it, and having it transcribed, I was able to use The Laugh Troubleshooter Process to identify opportunities to modify my delivery and see which laugh points I should keep and which ones still need work.

15.

The Writer's Block Eradicator™

What happens when you're stumped and don't know what to write about, or you're having a hard time thinking of something funny? To answer that common challenge, I am going to start by identifying, in my own experience, the reasons that a block happens. The primary reason why I've encountered writer's block is that I have placed some expectation on myself to produce a certain outcome. How is that for a vaguerality? Let me try again.

I sit down and look at a blank page and think to myself, "What is something funny that happened today?" Immediately, I have a problem because I run each moment of the day through the filter of "must be funny" before I even consider writing it down. Some examples of typical pieces of advice that can hinder creativity are that humor should further the story, make a point, or support your point. But, simply creating jokes and stories can be difficult on its own. Adding these extra constraints doubles or triples the difficulty.

> *Writer's block is a fancy term made up by whiners so they can have an excuse to drink alcohol.*
> **Steve Martin**

The first step to beat writer's block is to shed the burden of expectation. John Vorhaus advises us to lower our sights and expectations, forget outcomes, and focus on using the tools: require of yourself only that you do what you can do now. The following quote from *the little book of SITCOM* is an example of why I love John's writing, as he is so very pragmatic: "If you can't write, stop trying. Go gather data instead. Writing, you see, is a creative act. It engages our ego, which stalls our progress. Information gathering, on the other hand, leaves the ego alone, because information gathering is easy; there's no fear of failure."[131]

Gather data. Remember the basic idea behind The Laugh Generator Process? Get the facts and distort them. As Jerry Corley says, "Just write the truth, then turn it into something funny."[132] Remember the example of writing jokes about Amarillo in the previous chapter on The Material Machine? All I did was gather facts about Amarillo; that's all. Only later did I go back and take each fact through The Laugh Generator Process to develop a joke. Here's a summary of the process for beating writer's block based on Jerry Corley's and John Vorhaus's comic wisdom:

- Stop worrying about outcomes.
- Free-associate.
- Gather facts.
- Write the truth.

The final step to beat writer's block is to work towards developing a habit of writing. Scott Belsky, founder of Behance states, "Our individual practices ultimately determine what we do and how well we do it. Specifically, it's our routine (or lack thereof), our capacity to work proactively rather than reactively, and our ability to systematically optimize our work habits over time that determine our ability to make ideas happen."[133] Which brings us back to mindset. Steven Pressfield, author of the *War of Art*, describes "resistance" as "the enemy of the creative: Are you a writer who doesn't write, a painter who doesn't paint or an entrepreneur who never starts a venture? Then you know what resistance is."[134] *In Turning Pro*, Pressfield identifies that it's time to become a professional rather than an amateur and that transition is really about mindset:

> Turning pro is free, but it is not easy. You don't need to take a course or buy a product. All you have to do is change your mind.
>
> We can trade in the habits of the amateur and the addict for the practice of the professional and the committed artist or entrepreneur.[135]

James Clear is one of my favorite writers. He writes on a variety of topics and if you go to his website you will find he has a couple of books you can download for free, one on habits and the other on creativity. Obviously I think both habits and creativity apply to someone wanting to be funnier, so you should download and read both books. I started this book by stating that I read a lot of books. Do you believe me yet? Do you? In his book on creativity, James shares the secret to creativity is sticking to a strict schedule—not creative inspiration, which you might expect. And, no surprise, James discusses the differences between an amateur and a professional and what turning pro really means. Well worth your time.

I think I did pretty well, considering I started out with nothing but a bunch of blank paper.
Steve Martin

How to Do It

Earlier, I point out that a common mistake you might ask yourself is "What's funny?" Here's an example of this mistake posted on the National Speaker's Association Facebook group: "Does anyone have any good ideas for fun/humorous openers for a techie group when speaking about health & fitness?" So that's the question, "What's a funny opener for a techie group?" I didn't know. Nothing came to me immediately, which is common when starting out by asking, "What's funny?" But I knew the process. First, I don't worry about the outcome. Second, I free-associate. Third, I gather facts.

My first questions to the speaker who posted the question were: "What type of techie group? IT Helpdesk, Network support?" She replied, "Software developers in a software company." Now I have something more specific. Specifics and details are a good place to start. I started just like I do when I write jokes. I made two lists—one for Software/Software Company and one for Health and Fitness/Zumba. Why Zumba? I visited the speaker's website and discovered that she teaches Zumba. Again, find something specific. Whenever I create lists, I'm interested in key words, phrases, and clichés. I also look, in particular, for complete statements or facts. In this case, about 10 minutes into generating the lists and looking for statements or facts, I found a few phrases that sparked an idea.

Software Development	Health/Fitness/Zumba
Data-driven development	fun, easy to do, music gets you moving
Business requirements gathering	Brain thinks it's dancing; body thinks it's exercise
Deleted code is debugged code	Music is infectious
Quality assurance	Fun! It's different, it's effective
Adding more processors may not make the program run faster	Easy-to-follow moves
	You can't help but move to the beat and burn 300-800 calories at the same time
	You should wear loose, comfortable clothing
	You should always stretch at the beginning and end
	Do not wear running shoes or cross-trainers because they are designed for forward motion
	The music is infectious and makes you feel like you are in a Latin nightclub

This is what I posted for the speaker:

You could structure this like a game and could start by saying, "I have a list of things I say in my Zumba classes that probably apply to software development. You tell me."

- Fun, easy to do, music gets you moving
- Brain thinks it's dancing; body thinks it's exercise
- Music is infectious
- Fun! It's different, it's effective
- Easy-to-follow moves
- You can't help but move to the beat and burn 300–800 calories at the same time.

- You should wear loose, comfortable clothing
- You should always stretch at the beginning and end
- Adding more processors may not make the program run faster.

My only purpose for including this real example is to show you that the key to The Writer's Block Eradicator is to simply start writing. If I sat there thinking, "What's funny?" I would have never generated anything. However, I set my expectations aside, started writing down whatever came to mind for each topic (just like in The Simple Joke Writing System"), and in the process of writing down lists for each subject, I realized that some of the Zumba terms would be funny if they were applied to software development.

The only way to beat writer's block is to write. Really. In the case of writing or creating humor, you can just sit down and write your story. But since you are a speaker, speak your story. Once you do that, you have the facts. Now, walk through The Laugh Generator Process and make them funny. In this process, you must fight the resistance.

As Steven Pressfield wrote, "Resistance's goal is not to wound or disable. Resistance aims to kill."

One additional reason you may be facing writer's block is having too many options. In the example above, all I knew was techie and health/fitness. Those general concepts provided too many options. Once I narrowed each one down to software development and Zumba, my brain was able to start associating words, phrases and ideas. Using the Material Machine gives you a lot of options for humorous material. Unfortunately, a lot of options can cause a lack of momentum.

In James Clear's book *Mastering Creativity*, which you can download from his website (I probably already mentioned it so I really mean it. Download it!), he discusses how Dr. Seuss made a bet that resulted in one of his best-known works. Clear describes how Dr. Seuss made a $50 bet that he could write a children's book using only 50 different words. He won that bet and created the book, *Green Eggs and Ham*. If you find yourself facing writer's block and the above techniques haven't worked, it may be time to set some constraints. Maybe you join Toastmasters and commit to delivering a new humorous speech every month. That will require you to prepare and do the work. Bottom line, don't worry about the outcome; gather facts and do the work. Oh, and have fun! This is humor after all.

Resources

What Now?

That's it. This is where the teaching stops. So what now? That's actually up to you. Chances are you probably aren't any funnier if all you've done is read my book, unless reading is the optimal method for you for learning.

I'm in a Facebook group for an online course. A couple of days ago I saw this comment in the discussion: "If you're good doing the work with an online course then it may be for you! I'm finding out that live, in-person classes are really the best mode of learning for me." Now although I can work through an online course just fine, I tend to agree with this person's comment. I, too, do learn better via live instruction.

> *Progress is a natural result of staying focused on the process of doing anything.*
> **Thomas Sterner**

So the question for you is how do you learn best? If reading isn't optimal for you, there are other learning options available at my website, www.AFunnierYou.com, including an online course and opportunities for live, in-person training with me, too. Plus, you'll also get opportunities for coaching, both individual and group.

Another reason you probably aren't funnier yet is that you haven't begun using what you've learned. Or maybe you have. Without action, learning hasn't really occurred. That means that you must now begin to practice and apply your new knowledge. There's a big difference between learning and doing.

I once read a book on swimming. No, seriously, I did. About eight years ago I was considering taking up triathlons, and I knew that learning to actually swim (rather than knowing how to not drown) would be important. As is my nature, I bought a book on a swimming technique called Total Immersion. I read it but never practiced. Whenever I felt like swimming I remembered I'd have to wear a speedo. Nobody wants to see that. Hence, I'm no better at swimming than I was before I read the book.

I like how James Clear explains learning and practicing in this excerpt from his blog: "The state of your life right now is a result of the habits and beliefs that you have been practicing each day. When you realize this and begin to direct your focus toward practicing better habits day-in and day-out, continual progress will be the logical outcome."[136] And if you aren't convinced yet, here's a clip from an email I got from Derek Halpern, one of my teachers and mentors. You can read the email on his blog: socialtriggers.com/how-to-be-great/

People often think I'm a "natural" at speaking and at "being on video."

Well....

That couldn't be further from the truth.

You see, I became great at speaking and being on video because I wanted to become great at it.

I'd buy educational material to help me get better ... including online courses, books, and workshops.

I'd practice regularly ... including filming the same

video over and over and over again until I got it right.

And most important: I gave myself permission to be bad because I knew if I kept at it I'd get good....

How did I become great?

As I said....

I'd buy educational material. I'd practice. And most important, I'd give myself permission to be bad.

AND YOU NEED TO DO THE SAME.

No matter what you're trying to accomplish: invest in yourself, practice regularly, and give yourself permission to be bad.

And you'll thank me later.

At this point, you might be facing a lot of resistance and some self-doubt, As a reminder, the two biggest obstacles you'll face have to do with you: your mindset and your willingness to practice. To help you overcome the resistance, willingness, and mindset, I provide a very detailed outline of what to practice and how to practice in How to Become the Funniest You, which is coming up next.

When the proper mechanics of practice are understood, the task of learning something new becomes a stress-free experience of joy and calmness.
Thomas Sterner

To help you stay focused on the process of becoming funnier, I've also included The 90-Day Humor Improvement Plan after that. Although the plan takes 90 days, the amount of effort on any given day is not a lot. The whole point of the plan is that you work on practicing and developing the skills every day. If you follow the plan, I will certainly guarantee you will be a funnier you. From Daniel Coyle's blog: "It's not so much about your 'natural talents,' as it is about your mindset and your habits."[137]

You now have all the information and processes to help you generate laughs, troubleshoot them, multiply them, and get the most out of each one. You also know if you run the risk of offending anyone. Plus, you have specific information about how to practice and complete a 90-day plan of action.

But ... that may still not be enough. Human nature may still get in your way. You may tell yourself you'll start tomorrow. You'll give it a shot and try it out on your next speech. Or, maybe you've even decided that "being funny just isn't for me." If that is the case, please go back and recall why humor is a must in any speech! Now, commit to becoming an exceptional presenter. To achieve exceptional status, you probably need a coach or at least a group of like-minded people trying to accomplish the same thing. As Napoleon Hill said, "When a group of individual brains are coordinated and function in harmony, the increased energy created through that alliance becomes available to every individual brain in the group."[138] Yes, being in a training group with other like-minded people will pay off hugely.

Both of these—a coach and a group of like-minded people—are available for you at www.AFunnierYou.com.

Becoming the Funniest You

One of the major obstacles in your way to becoming a funnier you is practice. I hope you are on board and "all in" by now on the idea that practice is essential. Unfortunately, practice isn't simple. First, there is the willingness and second, there is actually knowing how to practice. In this resource, I'm going to simplify the practice process for you so you can get much funnier, much faster.

> *If I cannot persuade you to practice, I cannot help you to improve.*
> **Timothy Koegel**

The key to getting better is to practice, but not just any practice will do. The type of practice that will get you funnier fast is something called intentional practice, because you want to practice in a way that will get you much funnier, faster. I recommend you apply Daniel Coyle's REPS gauge to your practice sessions:[139]

R stands for Reaching/Repeating. Is the practice requiring you to reach the edges of your ability? How often?

E stands for Engagement. Does the practice have your attention? Are you engaged?

P stands for Purposefulness. Is your practice building the skill you want to develop?

S stands for Strong, Direct, Immediate Feedback. Do you have a way to know how you are doing?

Now that you have a way to measure the effectiveness of you practice, let's drill into each skill area and identify some specific ways to practice each one.

Practicing The Laugh Generator™ Process

Since The Laugh Generator Process is, in fact, a process, you should plan to practice it as a process in its entirety. What does that mean? If you currently have a speech or presentation that you would like to enhance with some more laughs, cool; take it through The Laugh Generator Process. Or since that may seem a bit overwhelming, consider isolating a five-minute portion of the speech and walking through the process with that smaller portion.

One additional way to add humor and to practice the process is to introduce a new personal story that you have used with the process. You can also practice the process by researching your current location, like I did with Amarillo.

Finally, you can practice with other people's speeches. You can enter "transcripts of famous speeches" into a search engine and be presented with an endless opportunity to practice. Also, TED Talks have transcripts available, too. You can also see the point where the audience laughs, which is nice. That's actually an understatement. Seeing the point where the audience laughs is an incredible opportunity and a powerful learning tool. Whichever way makes sense to you and seems like a good place to start, start there.

Next, while you are working on practicing the entire process, let's also practice the basics of using surprise to generate laughs. You will recall that using surprise involves two subskills. First, there is the ability to identify the assumed, expected meaning and then second, create a twist on the assumption and expectation to generate a laugh. Since these two skills are the heart of The Laugh Generator Process, the more you practice, the funnier you will be, and you will be able to identify laugh opportunities with greater ease. You can practice using surprise in the following ways:

1. Opportunities exist everywhere you go. Pay attention to what people say and see if you can identify possible ways to twist it. The nice thing is you don't have to say it out loud; you can keep it to yourself.
2. For example, the staff at the coffee shop like to say,

"What can I get started for you?" What is the assumed answer and what could be a possible twist?

3. Keep a notebook or the note app on your phone or computer available and jot these phrases down so you can practice them later.
4. In the section regarding ad-libs, I suggest that the best ad-lib is a prepared ad-lib! One way to practice generating surprise is to make a list of every situation that could happen during a speech and come up with 10 possible ad-libs.
5. For example, the lights go out. What is the upside? What is the downside? What is the literal interpretation? Why did they go out? Who is responsible?
6. Watch videos of your favorite comedians or late-night monologues. When the audience laughs, stop the video and write out the lines that made the audience laugh. You already know that Brian Kiley is one of my favorite comedians for this exercise. Watch him and you'll see why. His joke structure is impeccable.
7. Once you have the lines that generated the laugh, play a little game and see if you can come up with 10 alternative twists or punch lines.
8. This may seem like the same as above, but it's actually different. Rather than watching comedians, watch TED Talks and look at the transcript. In a search engine, enter your favorite TED Talk and transcript. For example, "TED Talk Sir Ken Robinson Transcript" without the quotes will get you the transcript of his very popular TED Talk.

Practicing the Simple Joke Writing System™

You can practice The Simple Joke Writing System in the following ways:
- By using the content of your speeches or presentations. You may have to introduce "What is this like?" to create a secondary element.
- By practicing with your actual speech or presentation content, you will be able to find joke possibilities in addition to the ones revealed using The Laugh Generator Process.
- By writing facts about yourself, about your day, about your life. I regularly practice by doing this. Remember, you don't start with funny; you start with truth and make it funny. One day as I was writing facts, I wrote this one: "We found three scorpions in our house this week." The twist that made this simple fact funny was by adding the comment, "One more, and we're forming a band."
- By using news headlines.
- By using OMG Facts or another factoid-type site or application. I typically look at OMG Facts Twitter feed: twitter.com/OMGFacts and see what catches my eye. Today, there are two items that I'll work on: "Everything You Thought You Knew About Younger Siblings Was A Lie" and "After You Read These 9 Facts You'll Sleep MUCH Better At Night"
- Use famous lines from movies or songs that are already familiar to a majority of people. For example, this line from Forrest Gump is a perfect choice: "Life is a like a box of chocolates." Everyone knows the next line: "You never know what you're going to get." So when you have an alternate second line, the surprise will be even greater.

Practicing The Laugh Multiplier™ Process

You can practice The Laugh Multiplier Process in the following ways:
1. I find that the more I know my own speech, the more likely I am to create a tag or topper in the moment. So whenever you are giving your speech, let your brain flow creatively.
2. In The Laugh Generator Process practice section, I recommended that you play a little game to see if you can come up with 10 alternate twists or punch lines. Now take those alternate twists and see if you can turn them into a tag or a topper. How about an act-out? Can you create multiple laughs from the initial laugh?
3. Do the same as above but with TED Talks or other speeches.
4. My favorite way to practice generating tags or toppers is to listen to comedians or funny speeches and in the moment, allow the creative act to happen. You may find you have a knack for creating tags and toppers this way as well.

Practicing Delivery and The Laugh Amplifier™

You can practice your delivery and The Laugh Amplifier in the following ways:
1. Probably the best way to practice is by being on stage and presenting. You can do that by going to storytelling events, signing up at open mic comedy nights, speaking at service clubs, or joining Toastmasters.
2. In your daily life, you will be telling stories and doing what people do—talking to other people. Make a note

to remind yourself to really practice your delivery and The Laugh Amplifier.
3. Watch comedians or speakers live in-person or on video. Pay attention to their delivery and make note of when the presenter could have benefited from a different delivery.
4. Likewise, watch people in everyday life. Watch the people at work or where you are a customer. How do they use delivery and is it effective? Do some people overdo facial expressions?

Practicing The Laugh Troubleshooter™ Process

The Laugh Troubleshooter Process has two parts that require practice. The first part is the inspection process to determine if you're providing too little or too much information. The second part is reconfiguring or reconstructing the joke to potentially fix the confusion or lack of information. You can practice The Laugh Troubleshooter Process in the following ways:

1. As you practice The Laugh Generator Process, you will have some jokes that work and others that don't. That is the entire reason The Laugh Troubleshooter Process exists. Use it and practice it.
2. Go to comedy open mics, watch amateur comedy shows, or watch YouTube videos. You will have a lot of opportunity to practice troubleshooting jokes.
3. Join Toastmasters and every meeting will provide you an opportunity to practice. You will have the opportunity to practice troubleshooting your own material and the other members' material too.

Practicing The Safe Humor Solution™

The foundation of The Safe Humor Solution is in knowing two key pieces of information about your jokes: target and subtext. You can practice The Safe Humor Solution in the following ways:
1. As you practice The Laugh Generator Process, take the extra step and identify the target and the subtext.
2. Watch speakers and comedians live and on YouTube. Identify the target and subtext of each joke or several jokes.
3. Late night talk shows are great opportunities to practice identifying the two elements. They tend to be very targeted and loaded with subtext.
4. The Comedy Central Roasts or even the old Dean Martin Roasts are specific events that are full of target jokes.

Practicing The Material Machine™

One of the most important skills is finding material or content you can use in your speeches and presentations. The Material Machine is designed to help you always have something funny to add or include. You can practice The Material Machine in the following ways:

1. Practice developing ad-lib jokes based on everything that can go wrong. Keep adding to the list and keep generating more material.
2. Keep a notebook (electronic or physical) and keep noting your daily events. Identify them, write facts about them, and then write jokes.
3. Each month, look up the national days of that month. Practice generating jokes based on that month.

4. Look at the news daily and identify a headline that captures your attention. Tie it to your speech and generate some jokes.
5. The list goes on and on. The whole point is to practice identifying all the opportunities for material.

The Habit of Practice

My comedy mentor Jerry Corley highly recommends getting into the habit of writing every day. In our case, consider writing every day to be practicing every day. He then went on to describe the Jerry Seinfeld idea of "not breaking the chain."

LifeHacker.com describes the process that Jerry Seinfeld shared with Brad Isaac, a young comic who asked for some advice:

> He said the way to be a better comic was to create better jokes and the way to create better jokes was to write every day.
>
> He told me to get a big wall calendar that has a whole year on one page and hang it on a prominent wall. The next step was to get a big red magic marker.
>
> He said for each day that I do my task of writing; I get to put a big red X over that day. "After a few days you'll have a chain. Just keep at it and the chain will grow longer every day. You'll like seeing that chain, especially when you get a few weeks under your belt. Your only job next is to not break the chain."
>
> "Don't break the chain," he said again for emphasis.[140]

In my experience, the only way to practice every day is to focus on the process, not on the outcomes. Which is why I love this quote from Daniel Coyle: "To get good, it's helpful to be willing, or even enthusiastic, about being bad. Baby steps are the royal road to skill."[141]

Step one to becoming the funniest you is regular practice. Step two is to make each practice count and push your limits.

You probably recall John Vorhaus's admonition to go for 10. For every 10 jokes, you write, 9 won't work, but that is how we get better.

> Becoming a master of karate was not about learning 4,000 moves, but about doing just a handful of moves 4,000 times.
> **Chet Holmes**

Gene Perret expands on that idea of setting a quota for yourself by sharing Drew Carey's advice on the subject: "You have to treat comedy—writing and performing—like a job. One of the ways I did that was to set minimums for myself— like writing ten jokes a day."[142]

The Case for Toastmasters

The only way to get better is by practicing. And in the case of humor, you want to practice before you have to be good. Toastmasters is an excellent place to do that.

The Toastmasters program is uniquely designed to put you in the position of having to practice. Each meeting provides you with many opportunities to practice laugh generation skills in front of a real audience. Each meeting has three sections. The first section is the formal speeches, the second section is impromptu speaking, and the third section is evaluations. In addition, each meeting has several additional roles that

will provide you opportunities to practice being funny in the moment. Beyond the meetings are the contests that provide an excellent method to "increase the stakes" as Tim Ferriss recommends in a *Fast Company* article:
1. Find places to fit in "No Stakes" practice.
2. Set up real stakes to guarantee follow-through.[143]

Twice a year in Toastmasters, you will have the opportunity to compete in speech contests. Although there is a specific contest for humorous speaking, each contest allows for humor and a lot of it. Competing in a contest is a great way to set up some real stakes for yourself. Every club meeting also provides you with plenty of opportunity for "no stakes" practice, too. In order to make a meeting successful, there are several roles that need to be filled. If you aren't officially speaking, you will have an opportunity to fill one of the following roles:

- Toastmaster
- Table Topics Host
- General Evaluator
- Speech Evaluator
- Table Topics Speaker

You can read about these roles on the Toastmasters' website, www.toastmasters.org/Membership/Club-Meeting-Roles. Once you join, you will be provided *The Competent Communicator* manual, which has your first 10 speech projects:
1. The Ice Breaker
2. Organize Your Speech
3. Get to the Point
4. How to Say It
5. Your Body Speaks
6. Vocal Variety
7. Research Your Topic
8. Get Comfortable with Visual Aids

9. Persuade with Power
10. Inspire Your Audience

The first project is your opportunity to introduce yourself to the club and is an excellent opportunity to write down facts about yourself. Then you can walk those facts through The Laugh Generator. Then you will be able to practice using The Laugh Amplifier techniques to deliver your speech. Finally, because you will record it and have it transcribed, you will then walk through The Laugh Troubleshooter process and The Laugh Multiplier. All of those opportunities come from your very first speech. From there, you can repeat the process.

The 10 projects will allow you to focus on and practice specific skills. For example, project four provides the added focus of word choice, vivid language, and specific rhetorical devices. You can practice similes, metaphors, and the rule of three. Project five is all about body language and is a perfect opportunity to focus on this specific skill set. Project six provides another opportunity to specifically focus some of the nonverbal qualities of your voice. Completing your first manual, *The Competent Communicator*, means you are ready to take on the advanced manual. Because Toastmasters is a well-structured program, you will have several advanced manuals to choose from.

Thanks to the variety of projects, you will be able to hone your humor skills while at the same time meeting other objectives, like speaking to inform or delivering a management briefing. Without a doubt, being an active member of Toastmasters will provide you with high REPS practice. You can read more about the Toastmaster programs here: www.toastmasters.org/Resources/Education-Program/Communication-Track.

Going Beyond Toastmasters

When it comes to practicing, beyond testing, the goal is to get closer to the real experience and environment. So while Toastmasters is a safe, fun place to test and play with your humor, they are a very generous audience. To really test your material, you need to take it another step. To do that, reach out to civic clubs such as Rotary, Kiwanis, and Lions Clubs. Each of them actively seeks speakers for their programs. Typically, you'll have 20 to 30 minutes on the program with 10 minutes of Q&A time.

To find these opportunities, simply enter your town or city name, followed by one of the service clubs I've listed above. From there, you will find a website that will include more information, including contact information for either the president of the club or the program director. Reach out to them regarding any open speaking spots. Mention that you are a speaker and that you are developing a new speech and would love to hear their feedback. The important point is to get started and keep practicing. It's fundamental whenever you want to be good at something.

The 90-Day Humor Improvement Plan™

The goal of The 90-Day Humor Improvement Plan is to provide an easy-to-follow plan to practice the essentials skills for becoming funnier onstage and off. The plan includes daily practice items along with practice items that are to be completed over a five-day period. Follow the plan and you will have practiced the entire process four times, which is enough times to get comfortable with the process.

Here are some things to keep in mind while you follow the plan:
- Daily practice of 15 to 20 minutes is better than 1 hour done weekly.
- Watch comedians and speakers, but don't do it passively. Actively devour the performance.
- Pay close attention to the performance: face, voice inflection, and mannerisms.
- Practice delivering the same lines the same way as the performer.
- There will be times when practicing is a real struggle. Embrace those times.
- Enhance your practice time by organizing each session into three specific periods with up to 10 minute breaks in between each block.
- Before you go to sleep each night, play a movie in your mind of your ideal humorous performance. And then have sheep be your audience and count them.

Daily Practice

Daily, for the next 90 days, listen to the words people say. Practice finding alternate or double meanings along with expectations and assumptions. Make a note of them and see if you can create a funny twist. In addition, watch a minimum of 10 minutes of your favorite comedian or speaker. Pay attention to the laughs. Make a note of the lines that make up the laugh. Try to top the comedian and generate additional twists for the comedian or speaker. Try to generate tags/toppers for the comedian or speaker. When possible, identify the target and the subtext in the jokes. Finally, look at the news headlines and make a note of the ones that interest you.

> *If people knew how hard I worked to gain my mastery, it would not seem so wonderful after all.*
> **Michelangelo**

Week 1

In addition to your daily practice, identify your best opportunities to practice. Toastmasters? Story nights? Nerd nights? Pick a story or a five- to seven-minute portion of your speech to take through the entire process.

Week 2

Keep going with your daily practice. Sometime this week, give your speech and record it. Have it transcribed. Walk through The Laugh Generator with your speech.

Week 3

Walk through The Laugh Amplifier and the Laugh Multiplier with your speech.

Week 4

Give your speech again, record it, and have it transcribed. Walk through The Laugh Troubleshooting Process.

Week 5

Using a news headline, walk through The Simple Joke Writing System process. Pick a couple of the items that can go wrong during a presentation and create ad-libs.

Week 6

Using a news headline, walk through The Simple Joke Writing System process. Pick a couple of the items that can go wrong during a presentation and create ad-libs.

Week 7

Pick another story or a 5- to 7-minute portion of your speech. Give your speech and record it. Have it transcribed. Walk through The Laugh Generator, The Laugh Amplifier, and The Laugh Multiplier with your speech.

Week 8

Using a news headline, walk through The Simple Joke Writing System process. Pick a couple of the items that can go wrong during a presentation and create ad-libs.

Week 9

Give your speech again, record it, and have it transcribed. Walk through The Troubleshooting Process.

Week 10

Using a news headline, walk through The Simple Joke Writing System process. Pick a couple of the items that can go wrong during a presentation and create ad-libs.

Week 11

Pick another story or a 5- to 7-minute portion of your speech. Give your speech and record it. Have it transcribed. Walk through The Laugh Generator, The Laugh Amplifier, and The Laugh Multiplier with your speech.

Week 12

Using a news headline, walk through The Simple Joke Writing System process. Pick a couple of the items that can go wrong during a presentation and create ad-libs.

Week 13

Give your speech again, record it, and have it transcribed. Walk through The Troubleshooting Process.

> *Talent is cheaper than table salt. What separates the talented individual from the successful one is a lot of hard work.*
> **Stephen King**

Congratulations! You've made it and have done what most people don't do: put in the time to practice. Now that you've completed the 90-Day Plan, the next step is to do it again. Will you do it for a Scooby Snack? Will you do it for two Scooby Snacks?

Author Biography

Rick Olson, an award-winning humorous speaker, has a background in IT, Direct Sales, Project Management, and Government and Insurance.

Although he was told all his life he was funny, no one was laughing when he gave stand-up comedy a shot. Being "naturally funny" failed him, so he was forced to figure it out or quit.

After years of intense study, Rick found an amazing coach and then committed hours of practice to his craft. Then Rick developed his Humor Toolkit to teach and coach his clients, so that they, too, can be "naturally funny." As a result, Rick's clients make more sales and become better speakers, better leaders, and more successful in whatever they do.

Notes

1. Timothy J. Koegel, The Exceptional Presenter: A Proven Formula to Open Up! and Own the Room (Austin, TX: Greenleaf Book Group Press, 2007), Kindle edition.
2. Mark Bowden, Tame the Primitive Brain: 28 Ways in 28 Days to Manage the Most Impulsive Behaviors at Work (Hoboken, NJ: John Wiley & Sons, 2013), 11-12.
3. Koegel, The Exceptional Presenter: A Proven Formula to Open Up! and Own the Room. Kindle edition.
4 "History of TED," TED: Ideas worth Spreading, www.ted.com/about/our-organization/history-of-ted.
5. Carmine Gallo, Talk like TED: The 9 Public Speaking Secrets of the World's Top Minds (New York: St. Martin's Press, 2014), 3-4.
6. Kim Lachance Shandrow, "The 5 Most Popular TED Talks of All Time," Entrepreneur, November 12, 2014. www.entrepreneur.com/article/239672.
7. Jenna Goudreau, "The Public Speaking Secret behind the Most Popular TED Talk of All Time," Business Insider, January 28, 2016, www.businessinsider.com/public-speaking-secret-of-most-popular-ted-talk-2016-1.
8. Carmine Gallo, The Storyteller's Secret: From TED Speakers to Business Legends, Why Some Ideas Catch on and Others Don't (New York, St. Martin's Press, 2016), 91.
9. Al Getler, "Sir Ken Robinson on Laughter," YouTube video, 3:01, a special lecture on February 2, 2013, posted by Al Getler, February 2, 2013, www.youtube.com/attribution?v=4q_FLaXA_BQ.

10. Gene Perret, How to Hold Your Audience with Humor: A Guide to More Effective Speaking (Cincinnati, OH: Writer's Digest Books, 1984), Foreword.
11. Daniel Coyle, "24 Rules for Becoming an Adult Prodigy," The Talent Code 24 Rules for Becoming an Adult Prodigy Comments, August 27, 2014, thetalentcode.com/2014/08/27/24-rules-for-becoming-an-adult-prodigy/.
12. David Robson, "Old Schooled: You Never Stop Learning like a Child," New Scientist, May 22, 2013, www.newscientist.com/article/mg21829181-800-old-schooled-you-never-stop-learning-like-a-child/.
13. Scott Adams, How to Fail at Almost Everything and Still Win Big: Kind of the Story of My Life. (New York, NY: Penguin Group, 2013, 69-70.
14. Daniel Coyle, The Talent Code: Greatness Isn't Born: It's Grown, Here's How (New York: Bantam Books, 2009), 94.
15. Tim Finnigan. "Mindset by Carol Dweck," Blockshelf - Lessons and Insights for Entrepreneurs, February 17, 2015, www.blockshelf.com/mindset-carol-dweck/.
16. Dan Gheesling, "Why You Need A Mentor to Be Successful, " Dan Gheesling, www.dangheesling.com/why-you-need-a-mentor/.
.17 Coyle, "24 Rules for Becoming an Adult Prodigy," The Talent Code 24 Rules for Becoming an Adult Prodigy Comments, August 27, 2014, thetalentcode.com/2014/08/27/24-rules-for-becoming-an-adult-prodigy/.
18. Darren LaCroix, "Lights, Camera, … HUMOR! The Rule of Three." Patricia Fripp, 2012, www.fripp.com/lights-camera-humor-the-rule-of-three/.

19. Timothy Ferriss, The 4-hour Chef: The Simple Path to Cooking like a Pro, Learning Anything, and Living the Good Life (Boston: New Harvest, 2012), Kindle edition.
20. Melvin Helitzer and Mark Shatz, Comedy Writing Secrets: The Best-selling Book on How to Think Funny, Write Funny, Act Funny, and Get Paid for It (Cincinnati, OH: Writer's Digest Books, 2005), Kindle edition.
21. Gene Perret, The Ten Commandments of Comedy (Fresno, CA: Quill Driver Books, 2013), Kindle edition.
22. Richard L. West and Lynn H. Turner, Understanding Interpersonal Communication: Making Choices in Changing Times (Belmont, CA: Thomson/Wadsworth, 2006), 198.
23. Vorhaus, The Comic Toolbox: How to Be Funny Even If You're Not. (Los Angeles: Silman-James Press, 1994), PAGE.
24. Jeffrey H. Gitomer, 21.5 Unbreakable Laws of Selling: Proven Actions You Must Take to Make Easier, Faster, Bigger Sales … Now and Forever. (Austin, TX, Bard Press, 2013), 38.
25. "Stress Is Killing You," The American Institute of Stress, www.stress.org/stress-is-killing-you/.
26. "Statistic Brain," Statistic Brain, Accessed June 17, 2016, www.statisticbrain.com/stress-statistics/.
27. Jeanne Segal, Ph.D., Melinda Smith, M.A., Robert Segal, M.A., and Lawrence Robinson, "Stress Symptoms, Signs, Causes, and Coping Tips," HealthGuide.org, www.helpguide.org/articles/stress/stress-symptoms-causes-and-effects.htm.

28. Bob Clark, "Laughter Provides Benefits for a Healthy Life," Tampa Bay Times, August 20, 2014, www.tampabay.com/news/health/laughter-provides-benefits-for-a-healthy-life/2193926.
29. Mayo Clinic Staff, "Stress Management." Stress Relief from Laughter? It's No Joke," www.mayoclinic.org/healthy-lifestyle/stress-management/in-depth/stress-relief/art-20044456.
30. Matt Abrahams, "Matt Abrahams: Tips and Techniques for More Confident and Compelling Presentations," Stanford Graduate School of Business, March 2, 2015, www.gsb.stanford.edu/insights/matt-abrahams-tips-techniques-more-confident-compelling-presentations.
31. "Brain Rules: Brain Rules for Meetings," Brain Rules: Brain Rules for Meetings, January 30, 2012, brainrules.blogspot.com/2012/01/brain-rules-for-meetings.html.
32. Sam Horn, Got Your Attention?: How to Create Intrigue and Connect with Anyone. (Oakland, CA: Berrett-Koehler Publishers, 2015), 1.
33. "Hilarious Southwest Flight Attendant," YouTube video, 03:06, April 12, 2014, www.youtube.com/watch?v=07LFBydGjaM.Marty Cobb Smile High Club.
34. James Altucher, "11 Unusual Methods for Being a Great Public Speaker," Altucher Confidential, June 2011, www.jamesaltucher.com/2011/06/11-unusual-methods-for-being-a-great-public-speaker/.
35. "Use This 2-part Formula to Rock Any Introduction in 60 Seconds," Ziglar Vault, August 21, 2015, June 17, 2016. ziglarvault.com/use-this-2-part-formula-to-rock-any-introduction-in-60-seconds/.

36. Jeffrey Gitomer, "A Lesson from a Laugh. Listen to This One-Column Archive," Buy Gitomer, 2016, gitomer.com/articles/ViewPublicArticle. html?key=ajcdMibak3Mch4wswv/MWQ==#sthash. kit5IKbm.dpuf.
37. Zak H. Stambor, "How Laughter Leads to Learning." American Psychological Association, June 2006, www.apa.org/monitor/jun06/learning.aspx.
38. Honor Whiteman, "Seniors / Aging Neurology / Neuroscience Alzheimer's / Dementia Anxiety / Stress Is Laughter the Best Medicine for Age-related Memory Loss?" Medical News Today, April 28, 2014, www.medicalnewstoday.com/articles/276042.php.
39. Nancy Recker, "Laughter Is Really Good Medicine," PDF, Ohio State University Extension, 2007, www.dartmouth.edu/~eap/library/Laughter_Good_Medicine.pdf
40. Martha Burns, Ph.D.,"Dopamine and Learning: What The Brain's Reward Center Can Teach Educators, " Scientific Learning, September 18, 2012, www.scilearn.com/blog/dopamine-learning-brains-reward-center-teach-educators.
41. Ananya Mandal, MD, "Dopamine Functions," News-Medical.net., October 27, 2015, www.news-medical.net/health/Dopamine-Functions.aspx.
42. Kevan Lee, "How to Harness Your Brain's Dopamine Supply and Increase Motivation," Lifehacker, January 08, 2014, lifehacker.com/how-to-harnass-your-brains-dopamine-supply-and-increas-1496989326

43. Therese J. Borchard, "9 Ways That Humor Heals | World of Psychology," World of Psychology, February 17, 2009, psychcentral.com/blog/archives/2009/02/17/9-ways-that-humor-heals/.
44. Bob Burg, "All Things Being Equal ...," Bob Burg, April 12, 2010, www.burg.com/2010/04/all-things-being-equal.
45. Jeffrey H. Gitomer, "A Little Humor Can Go a Long Way in Sales," Long Island Business News, June 30, 2000, libn.com/2000/06/30/a-little-humor-can-go-a-long-way-in-sales/.
46. Jeffrey H. Gitomer, 21.5 Unbreakable Laws of Selling: Proven Actions You Must Take to Make Easier, Faster, Bigger Sales ... Now and Forever! (Bard Press, 2013), 40.
47. Ken, Ley, "Are You Laughing Enough at Work?" Ley's Jam, October 5, 2013, www.leys.dk/are-you-laughing-enough-at-work/.
48. Brad Larsen, "10 Reasons a Sense of Humor Is No Laughing Matter," Standard-Examiner, March 26, 2015, www.standard.net/Success-Strategies/2015/03/26/10-reasons-a-sense-of-humor-is-no-laughing-matter.
49. Deborah Swallow, "How Humour in Negotiations Increases Sales 15%, Deborah Swallow, Leading Authority on Intercultural Communication, April 19, 2010, www.deborahswallow.com/2010/04/19/how-humour-in-negotiations-increases-sales-15/.
50. Perri O. Blumberg, "Reader's Digest Trust Poll: Here's What Shocked Us the Most | Reader's Digest." Readers Digest, Access, www.rd.com/culture/readers-digest-trust-poll-heres-what-shocked-us-the-most/.

51. Peter Sims, "In On The Joke: Collaboration Through Humor," Fast Company, April 22, 2011, www.fastcompany.com/1749246/joke-collaboration-through-humor.
52. Jonah Lehrer, "The Mirror Neuron Revolution: Explaining What Makes Humans Social," Scientific American, July 1, 2008, August 08, 2016. www.scientificamerican.com/article/the-mirror-neuron-revolut/.
53. Daniel Goleman and Richard E. Boyatzis, "Social Intelligence and the Biology of Leadership," Harvard Business Review, September 2008, hbr.org/2008/09/social-intelligence-and-the-biology-of-leadership/ar/.
54. Joe Polish and Dean Jackson, "Sean Stephenson on Becoming a Highly Paid Speaker—#175. "I Love Marketing," Podcast audio, 01:13:11, Oct. 20, 2014. ilovemarketing.com/seanstephenson-on-becoming-a-highly-paid-speaker/.
55. Grant Baldwin. "How to Get Speaking Engagements - The Speaker Lab." The Speaker Lab RSS2. May 09, 2016. thespeakerlab.com/get-speaking-engagements/.
56. Bob Hooey. Speaking for Success: Adding Mastery to Your Message; and Power to Your Presentation. (Egremont, AB: Success Publications, 2013), 64.
57. Alan Weiss, Million Dollar Speaking: The Professional's Guide to Building Your Platform (New York: McGraw-Hill, 2011), Kindle edition.
58. Judy Carter, The Message of You: Turn Your Life Story into a Money-making Speaking Career (New York: St. Martin's Press, 2013,) 228.
59. Jess Ekstrom, "10 Ways to Become a Paid Speaker," Entrepreneur, September 25, 2015, www.entrepreneur.com/article/248821.

60. Steve Gilliland, 40 Irrefutable Steps to Building a Substantial Speaking Business (Charleston, SC: Advantage Media Group, 2014), Kindle edition.
61. Gene Perret, The New Comedy Writing Step by Step: Revised and Updated with Words of Instruction, Encouragement, and Inspiration from Legends of the Comedy Profession (Sanger, CA: Quill Driver Books/Word Dancer Press, 2007), 158.
62. Dick Vosburgh, "Phyllis Diller: Raucous Comic Famous for Her Withering One-liners," The Independent, August 21, 2012, www.independent.co.uk/news/obituaries/phyllis-diller-raucous-comic-famous-for-her-withering-one-liners-8069891.html.
63. Judy Carter, The Comedy Bible: From Stand-up to Sitcom: The Comedy Writer's Ultimate How-to-guide (New York: Fireside, 2001), Kindle edition.
64. Corley, Breaking Comedy's DNA—The Breakthrough Comedy Writing System,128.
65. Helitzer and Shatz, Comedy Writing Secrets: The Best-selling Book on How to Think Funny, Write Funny, Act Funny, and Get Paid for It , Kindle edition.
66. Robinson, Ken, "Do Schools Kill Creativity?" (speech, TED Talk Subtitles and Transcript | TED.com, February 16, 2017), http://www.ted.com/talks/ken_robinson_says_schools_kill_creativity/transcript?language=en.
67. Corley, Breaking Comedy's DNA—The Breakthrough Comedy Writing System, 130.
68. Judy Carter, The Message of You: Turn Your Life Story into a Money-making Speaking Career (New York: St. Martin's Press, 2013,) 246.
69. Robinson, "Do Schools Kill Creativity?" . . .

70. Corley, Breaking Comedy's DNA—The Breakthrough Comedy Writing System, 150.
71. James Altucher, "How to Be the Best Public Speaker on the Planet." Altucher Confidential, October 07, 2013, www.jamesaltucher.com/2013/10/how-to-be-the-best-public-speaker-on-the-planet/.
72. Nathan Furr, Nathan, "How Failure Taught Edison to Repeatedly Innovate," Forbes, June 9, 2011, www.forbes.com/sites/nathanfurr/2011/06/09/how-failure-taught-edison-to-repeatedly-innovate/#303972f738f5.
73. Jerry Corley, "Biggest Mistakes Comedians Make When Writing Comedy," Stand Up Comedy Clinic, 2011, www.standupcomedyclinic.com/biggest-mistakes-comedians-make-when-writing-comedy/.
74. Sergiu Floroaia, "Gene Perret—Interview: 'The Secret' to Winning an Emmy for Comedy Writing," Punchline, April 29, 2015, punchline.ro/2015/04/29/gene-perret-interview-the-secret-to-winning-an-emmy-for-comedy-writing/.
75. Coyle, The Little Book of Talent: 52 Tips for Improving Skills, 106.
76. Sims, Little Bets: How Breakthrough Ideas Emerge from Small Discoveries, 1.
77. Jerry Corley, Breaking Comedy's DNA—The Breakthrough Comedy Writing System. (Burbank, CA, Jerry Corley, 2012), 24,
78. Ibid.
79. Koegel, The Exceptional Presenter: A Proven Formula to Open Up! and Own the Room, Kindle edition.

80. Steven Benna, "5 Nonverbal Communication Cues All Great Speakers Have Mastered," Business Insider, July 23, 2015, www.businessinsider.com/nonverbal-communication-public-speaking-2015-7.
81. Susan Weinschenk, "Five Things You Need to Know About People to Give a Better Presentation," Peachpit: Publishers of Technology Books, EBooks, and Videos for Creative People, September 12, 2012, www.peachpit.com/articles/article.aspx?p=1943944.
82. Laurie Guest, CSP, "What I Learned by Watching 15 Speakers in 2015," What I Learned by Watching 15 Speakers in 2015. 2016, www.solutionsarebrewing.com/ebooks/1/what-i-learned.html 8-9.
83. Andrew Newberg, M.D, and Mark Waldman, "The 8 Key Elements of Highly Effective Speech," Psychology Today, July 10, 2012, www.psychologytoday.com/blog/words-can-change-your-brain/201207/the-8-key-elements-highly-effective-speech.
84. Sarah Bourassa, "Ever Felt 'happily Disgusted'? Computer Maps 21 Distinct Facial Expressions," TODAY.com, March 21, 2014, www.today.com/health/ever-felt-happily-disgusted-computer-maps-21-distinct-facial-expressions-2D79452326.
85. Susan Weinschenk, 100 Things Every Presenter Needs to Know about People (Berkeley, CA: New Riders, 2012), 110.
86. Ibid., 164.
87. Vanessa Van Edwards, "20 Hand Gestures You Should Be Using—Science of People," Science of People, August 21, 2015, www.scienceofpeople.com/2015/08/20-hand-gestures-using/.

88. Craig Valentine and Mitch Meyerson, World Class Speaking: The Ultimate Guide to Presenting, Marketing and Profiting like a Champion (Garden City, NY: Morgan James, 2009), 141-142.
89. Stephen Hoover, The Joke's on You: How to Write Comedy (United States: Stephen Hoover, 2013), 61-63 and 152.
90. Susan Weinschenk, How to Get People to Do Stuff: Master the Art and Science of Persuasion and Motivation (Berkeley, CA: New Riders, 2013), 23.
91. Koegel, The Exceptional Presenter: A Proven Formula to Open Up! and Own the Room, PAGE.
92. Helitz and Shatz, Comedy Writing Secrets: The Best-selling Book on How to Think Funny, Write Funny, Act Funny, and Get Paid for It, Kindle edition.
93. Vorhaus,, Comedy Writing 4 Life, Kindle edition.
94. Carol S. Dweck, Mindset: The New Psychology of Success (New York: Random House, 2006), 5.
95. Meg Grant, "Will Smith Interview | Reader's Digest," Readers Digest, December 06, 2006, www.rd.com/advice/relationships/will-smith-interview/.
96. "MINDSET," Mindset, mindsetonline.com/whatisit/about/index.html.
97. Daniel Goleman, The Brain and Emotional Intelligence: New Insights, (Northampton, MA: More Than Sound, 2011), Kindle edition.
98. Brain HQ, "Implicit Memory," Brain HQ, 2015, www.brainhq.com/brain-resources/memory/types-of-memory/implicit-memory.
99. David Eagleman, Incognito: The Secret Lives of the Brain (New York: Pantheon Books, 2011), 57-59.

100. Bradford Evans, "Read Advice Louis C.K. Gave to an 18-Year-Old Standup in 2005," Splitsider, September 23, 2013, splitsider.com/2013/09/read-advice-louis-c-k-gave-to-an-18-year-old-standup-in-2005/.
101. Peter Sims, Little Bets: How Breakthrough Ideas Emerge from Small Discoveries (New York: Free Press, 2011) 2.
102. Jonah Weiner, "Jerry Seinfeld Intends to Die Standing Up," New York Times, December 20, 2012, www.nytimes.com/2012/12/23/magazine/jerry-seinfeld-intends-to-die-standing-up.html?_r=0.
103. Helitzer and Shatz, Comedy Writing Secrets: The Best-selling Book on How to Think Funny, Write Funny, Act Funny, and Get Paid for It, Kindle edition.
104. Jerry Corley, "3 Vital Things To Remember When Performing Stand-up Comedy—Stand Up Comedy Clinic," Stand Up Comedy Clinic, March 14, 2014, www.standupcomedyclinic.com/3-vital-things-to-remember-when-performing-stand-up-comedy/.
105. Peter McGraw and Joel Warner, The Humor Code: A Global Search for What Makes Things Funny (New York, NY, Simon and Schuster, 2015), 6.
106. Corley, Breaking Comedy's DNA - The Breakthrough Comedy Writing System, 22-23.
107. Helitzer and Shatz. Comedy Writing Secrets: The Best-selling Book on How to Think Funny, Write Funny, Act Funny, and Get Paid for It, Kindle edition.
108. Carter, The Message of You: Turn Your Life Story into a Money-making Speaking Career, 238.

109. Eric Markowitz, "Brilliant Leaders Use This Type of Humor (Hint: Think Woody Allen)," Inc.com, May 21, 2013, www.inc.com/magazine/201306/eric-markowitz/humor-self-deprecation-leaders.html.
110. "Joe Polish Presentation on Gary Halbert." YouTube video posted from Dan Kennedy SuperConference. YouTube. November 19, 2011, youtu.be/q4WotUTjLJY?t=17m36s. TRIED TO ACCESS LINK TO FIND OUT TIME LENGTH, BROKEN LINK.
111. Kenza Moller, "Research Brief: For Great Leaders, the Joke's on Them," Smith School of Business, June 17, 2013, smith.queensu.ca/insight/articles/research_brief_for_great_leaders_the_joke_s_on_them.
112. Dan Pink, "The Puzzle of Motivation," TedTalk video, 18:36, July 2009, August 08, 2016. www.ted.com/talks/dan_pink_on_motivation?language=en.
113. "Ronald Reagan - Our Noble Vision: An Opportunity for All." Reagan 2020 -. March 2, 1984, reagan2020.us/speeches/Our_Noble_Vision.asp.
114. Scott Dikkers, How to Write Funny: Your Serious Step-by-step Blueprint for Creating Incrediby, Irresistibly, Successfully Hilarious Writing (Chicago, IL, Scott Dikkers, 2014), Kindle edition.
115. Carter, The Message of You: Turn Your Life Story into a Money-making Speaking Career, 238.
116. Fred E. Miller, No Sweat Public Speaking!: How to Develop, Practice, and Deliver a Knock Your Socks off Presentation with No Sweat! (St. Louis, MO: Fred, 2011), 52.

117. Fred E. Miller, "Fred Miller Introduction," No Sweat Public Speaking, February 2012, nosweatpublicspeaking.com/wp-content/uploads/2012/02/Fred Miller's Introduction.pdf.
118. "Remarks at a White House Reception for the National Association of Elementary School Principals and the National Association of Secondary School Principals," www.reaganlibrary.archives.gov/archives/speeches/1983/72983c.htm.
119. Harold Key,"Think and Grin." Boys Life, March 1957, 78.
120. Patrick Snow. "Finding, Creating & Delivering a World-Class Speech." Interview by Bryan Caplovitz. SpeakerMatch. November 5, 2015. www.speakermatch.com/radio/119/finding-creating-delivering-a-world-class-speech/.
121. Steve Rizzo, "The Psychology of Laughter in Business," World's Funniest Motivational Business Speaker Steve Rizzo, February 17, 2016, www.steverizzo.com/the-psychology-of-laughter-in-business/.
122. Lisa Cron, Wired for Story: The Writer's Guide to Using Brain Science to Hook Readers from the Very First Sentence (New York: Ten Speed Press, 2012), Kindle edition.
123. Jenna Goudreau,"The Public Speaking Secret behind the Most Popular TED Talk of All Time," Business Insider, January 28, 2016, Augu www.businessinsider.com/public-speaking-secret-of-most-popular-ted-talk-2016-1.
124. Zig Ziglar, "Biscuits, Fleas and Pump Handles." YouTube video, 1:09:09, October 8, 2013, August 08, 2016, youtu.be/FxhU-Zkzfpo?t=51m6s.

125. John Cantu, "Comics and Their Writers: Mistakes Newbies Make." "Backstage Pass," HumorMall.com, www.johncantu.com/backstagepass/newbies-mistakes.html.
126. Alan Weiss, Million Dollar Speaking: The Professional's Guide to Building Your Platform (New York: McGraw-Hill, 2011), PAGE.
127. Laurie Guest, CSP, "What I Learned by Watching 15 Speakers in 2015." What I Learned by Watching 15 Speakers in 2015. 2016. www.solutionsarebrewing.com/ebooks/1/what-i-learned.html
128. Weiss, Million Dollar Speaking: The Professional's Guide to Building Your Platform, PAGE.
129. Guest, "What I Learned by Watching 15 Speakers in 2015." What I Learned by Watching 15 Speakers in 2015. 2016, Accessed August 07, 2016, 9.
130. Weiss, Million Dollar Speaking: The Professional's Guide to Building Your Platform. Kindle edition.
131. Vorhaus, The Little Book of Sitcom, 8
132. Jerry Corley, "Comedy Is Truth, " Stand Up Comedy Clinic, June 13, 2012, www.standupcomedyclinic.com/comedy-is-truth/.
133. Jocelyn K. Glei, Scott Belsky, Mark McGuinness, Gretchen Rubin, Seth Godin, Tony Schwartz, Leo Babauta, Cal Newport, Christian Jarrett, Erin Rooney Doland, Aaron Dignan, Lori Deschene, James Victore, Todd Henry, Scott McDowell, Stefan Sagmeister, Elizabeth Grace Saunders, and Steven Pressfield, Manage Your Day-to-day: Build Your Routine, Find Your Focus, and Sharpen Your Creative Mind (Las Vegas, NV: Amazon Publishing, 2013), 17,

134. Steven Pressfield, The War of Art: Break through the Blocks and Win Your Inner Creative Battle (New York: Black Irish Entertainment, 2012), Kindle edition.
135. Steven Pressfield, Turning Pro: Tap Your Inner Power and Create Your Life's Work (New York, NY: Black Irish Entertainment, 2012), 5, 20.
136. James Clear, "Stop Thinking and Start Doing: The Power of Practicing More." James Clear, 2015, jamesclear.com/learning-vs-practicing.
137. Daniel Coyle, "24 Rules for Becoming an Adult Prodigy," The Talent Code 24 Rules for Becoming an Adult Prodigy Comments, August 27, 2014, thetalentcode.com/2014/08/27/24-rules-for-becoming-an-adult-prodigy/.
138. Napoleon Hill, "Napoleon Hill Books | Read Online or Download in PDF," Napoleon Hill Books Read Online or Download in PDF, napoleonhill-books.com/think-and-grow-rich/chapter-10-power-of-the-master-mind-the-driving-force/.
139. Daniel Coyle, "A Gauge for Measuring Effective Practice," The Talent Code A Gauge for Measuring Effective Practice Comments, May 31, 2011, thetalentcode.com/2011/05/31/a-gauge-for-measuring-effective-practice/.
140. Gina Trapani, "Jerry Seinfeld's Productivity Secret." Lifehacker, July 24, 2007, lifehacker.com/281626/jerry-seinfelds-productivity-secret.
141. Daniel Coyle, The Talent Code: Greatness Isn't Born: It's Grown, Here's How (New York: Bantam Books, 2009), 94.
142. Gene Perret, "Writing to a Quota." Writing to a Quota., www.writersstore.com/writing-to-a-quota/.

143. Drake Baer. "Tim Ferriss Will Teach You How To Quickly Master Any Skill," *Fast Company*, June 14, 2013, www.fastcompany.com/3012955/dialed/tim-ferriss-will-teach-you-how-to-quickly-master-any-skill.

www.ingramcontent.com/pod-product-compliance
Lightning Source LLC
Chambersburg PA
CBHW050534300426
44113CB00012B/2088